RESTAURANT profits THROUGH advertising and promotion: the indispensable plan

Tom Feltenstein

with Joe Lachmuth

CBI

A CBI Book
Published by Van Nostrand Reinhold Company

dedicATioN

To my wife, Sherry, my son, Andrew, and my
daughter, Jennifer, who supported this endeavor
during an equally busy period in our life,
which included the start up of a new business.
You made it all possible.

CONTENTS

foreword

It's not too often that a large corporation's chairman, president, executives, and directors will invite an outsider to guide them through days of strategic planning.

But then it's not often that you can find a man of Tom Feltenstein's background. . . President of his own Restaurant Marketing Company. . . Marketing Manager for the world's largest fast-food firms. . . Senior Vice President of a major advertising agency.

Tom Feltenstein is a bit unorthodox and consistently strategic. He has successfully applied his analytical planning and development talent to food service companies whose major products run the gamut from roast beef to donuts. I know, first hand, that that gamut also includes chicken.

With Tom Feltenstein in your corner, you'll be able to face even the big officially-crowned champions and win!

Tom plays in marketing's major leagues. When he's pitching for you, the competition had better watch out. His book is a real hummer of a fast ball.

Lamar D. Berry
Vice President
Popeyes Famous Fried Chicken, Inc.
Advertising/Marketing

acknowledgments

My career as a restaurant marketing executive and consultant has firmly convinced me that restaurant sales wars are ultimately won in the trenches.

I have long been concerned that too many restaurant operators enter these wars without a battle plan. That is why I've written this book—to put them on equal footing with their competition. It is a task I've enjoyed thoroughly and it has been a pleasure to collaborate with one of my former associates, Joe Lachmuth, who brought the insight of his experience to bear on the problems of promoting restaurant business.

Together we want to express our appreciation to Gene Grennan, whose writing skills helped us to organize our thoughts and to express them clearly to our readers. We thank Eileen Walsh Grennan for her substantive editorial assistance, and her patience.

Finally, we all want to thank Kathy Savago, associate production editor at CBI, for helping us bring these efforts together in a format that is both attractive and practical.

Tom Feltenstein
Omaha, Nebraska
September 15, 1982

iNTRodUCTioN

Not too long ago, excellent facilities, product quality, and competitive pricing—plus a good location—almost guaranteed a restaurant operator profitable sales volume.

But today's highly competitive and inflationary environment has created a much more knowledgeable and value-oriented consumer. To sufficiently capture a significant share of your market, you must extend your restaurant's positive image into the local trading area and create enduring consumer loyalty for your restaurant.

Neighborhood-restaurant marketing is your vehicle for accomplishing this. It's your competitive edge for achieving higher sales. This book offers you the principles and practices you will need to utilize this important sales building process. The rest is up to you. It takes *commitment*. That's one thing this book cannot provide and which you must. *Commitment* is necessary to follow the disciplined process of neighborhood-restaurant marketing, from filling out the charts in the Situation Analysis to realistically isolating your strengths and weaknesses, to setting your objectives, and to creating your plan, to evaluating your results, and, eventually to tallying higher profits.

Those who embrace neighborhood-restaurant marketing will be rewarded with higher sales volume, greater customer counts, and stronger customer loyalty. It's all there for you *if* you just make the commitment to go for it!

Studies indicate that six out of every ten people who read this book will put it on the shelf and never implement its instructions. Four will really profit. Which group do you belong to? Which does your competition belong to?

Remember, you're in business to be the best. Neighborhood-restaurant marketing can make the difference between being the best and barely surviving.

So, good luck and good marketing!

restaurant profits through advertising and promotion: the indispensable plan

WHAT is NEiGHbORHOOD-RESTAURANT MARKetiNG?

CHAPTER ONE

IS your restaurant getting all the business it can? Is the competition putting the pressure on instead of running scared? Does the nearby competitor with obviously inferior food products and service get more business than it should? Are you tapping the true potential of the customer base surrounding your restaurant or restaurants?

It's highly likely that these questions have come up in some form or another. Perhaps you've had a vague feeling of uneasiness or a definite feeling that the cash register drawers aren't as full as they might be. If so, this book can help you improve business in the near future and for years to come.

The foundation of what will be taught is really a rather simple idea that has been around for a long time. Selling has always been an art, but in the last couple of generations it has developed into a disciplined science. It's my intention to help you put that discipline to work for you.

The idea I'm referring to has been known by many names. In the latest stages of its evolution it has been called local store marketing, community merchandising, store level area marketing, and neighborhood targeting, among other things. In this book, for reasons to be elaborated on later, this idea is called *neighborhood-restaurant marketing*.

Before we go any further, be assured of one thing: When the term "marketing" is used, it should not be taken to mean the complicated and costly techniques that can only be put into practice by batteries of business school graduates. In this book, marketing means the hands-on mechanics that can be performed by a limited staff at low cost. Most important, it means actions that produce sales.

The basic idea of neighborhood-restaurant marketing has been around for centuries. However, it has been refined in recent years, notably through the concentrated efforts of those foremost examples of successful restaurant marketing—McDonald's and Burger King. As a marketing executive for these two fast-food giants, I took part in developing the programs that still keep customers flocking to their outlets while the sales and growth of top competitors languish by comparison. So, I've learned what makes neighborhood-restaurant marketing work, and I'm going to pass that knowledge on to you.

Don't throw up your hands or shut this book thinking "Those guys have millions to spend and I'm not in that class." True, both firms lavish money on national and regional advertising. But what gives real strength to their sales is their insistence that individual restaurant operators engage in daily battle on localized fields. An understanding of neighborhood-restaurant marketing will arm you to succeed in the same type of competitive struggle.

A variety of economic facts and factors have combined to dramatically sharpen the importance of neighborhood-restaurant marketing, rendering its impact on sales even more explosive.

Consider:

- Seventy-five to eighty percent of most restaurant customers come from within three miles (or ten minutes) of each restaurant.
- High gasoline costs have caused more consumers to eat and shop closer to home.

- Since inflation has eroded purchasing power, consumers have become more diligent about securing greater value for their dollar.
- Inflation has made it imperative that restaurateurs make the most of their resources in generating sales traffic—that they get the best possible return on their investment for promoting business.
- Competition for the "neighborhood disposable dollar" has become tougher every day.
- A very small percentage of customers accounts for a very large percentage of total business.

Understanding this new business climate, and its particular implications for your own business, is crucial to continuing a profitable business.

NEIGHBORHOOD-RESTAURANT MARKETING DEFINED

Large companies allocate millions of dollars to their marketing programs. For the most part, those funds are channeled into three general tiers or levels of marketing.

The first of these tiers is national advertising. This is the province of firms like McDonald's, Burger King, or companies outside the restaurant industry who consider the entire country (or the world, for that matter) their market. This advertising, prepared by highly professional agencies, is what is seen on prime time television or in national magazines like *Newsweek, People, Fortune,* or *Forbes.* Its main intent is to establish the prestige of these companies, to make their names and reputations "household words." *This is not neighborhood-restaurant marketing.*

The second tier of marketing is regional in scope. This type of marketing, although it may benefit from the fallout from national campaigns, is more focused. Its targets are narrower, confined to specific groups of states or major metropolitan areas. It may concentrate on the sales of particular products. This type of marketing also requires large expenditures of funds for professional advertising on billboards, on radio, and in newspapers. *This is not neighborhood-restaurant marketing.*

The third tier of marketing is aimed directly at the person who comes into a store and pays money for the products offered. The focus of this marketing is on the three-to-five mile area that surrounds a store or group of stores. Some large companies either ignore this type of marketing altogether or pay it scant attention. The neighborhood restaurateur cannot afford such neglect (it probably costs the large companies money too!). He or she must mine the potential in that three-to-five mile trading area for all it's worth, since success will ultimately depend on the sales received from this area. *This, in essence, is neighborhood-restaurant marketing.*

To be more explicit, neighborhood-restaurant marketing essentially requires that you develop a keen awareness of anything in a trading area that can provide an opportunity to promote business. Now you will be shown how to recognize these opportunities and how to exploit them.

NEIGHBORHOOD-RESTAURANT MARKETING AND YOUR TRADING AREA

The trading area has already been defined geographically as the three-to-five mile (or ten-minute drive) locale that encircles a restaurant.

This physical area is the focal point of neighborhood-restaurant marketing. However, neighborhood-restaurant marketing requires more than studying a map. It demands careful and continual consideration of all the characteristics of the community surrounding your restaurant.

For instance, the trading area or community probably comprises various types of residential and business sections. There may be private homes, apartments, manufacturing concerns, and retail stores. Beyond that there may be supporting institutions: churches, grammar schools, high schools, service clubs, charities, social agencies, fire and police departments, city or town administrations.

Neighborhood-restaurant marketing means regarding each of these community components as potential sources of business. Neighborhood-restaurant marketing also means separating those people who occupy those residences, work in those factories or stores, attend those schools, perform social work—senior citizens, heads of families, men, women, boys, girls—into groupings that may be used as targets for marketing your restaurant.

Moreover, you must learn to view each of the community institutions as ways of promoting business. The restaurant must be regarded as a media center that is constantly sending out messages to those who live, work, and shop in your trading area—messages of good will, good quality, good service, good value, good citizenship, of a good place to eat.

This continual interaction between you, the restaurant, and all the elements of the trading area is the foundation of neighborhood-restaurant marketing. Its more visible structure consists of a disciplined series of advertising, promotion, community, and public relations activities. This book is a do-it-yourself blueprint for building this structure and for building sales and profits as well.

WHAT NEIGHBORHOOD-RESTAURANT MARKETING DOES FOR YOU

To raise the level of sales, you must accomplish at least one of these three basic goals:

1. Attract new customers.
2. Increase the number of "visits" by existing customers.
3. Increase the average amount per purchase at your restaurant.

Neighborhood-restaurant marketing is successful because it disciplines the restaurant owner/manager to concentrate his or her efforts, like a powerful laser beam, on this tried and true trio of marketing objectives. No matter how complex or sophisticated any marketing program becomes, it can be stripped down to new customers, more visits, higher transactions.

The astounding force of these simple truths can be expressed concretely: Let's see what they can mean to you.

Assume that your restaurant handles 6,000 transactions a week, with each transaction averaging $3.00, adding up to weekly sales of $18,000. Because an average restaurant trading area consists of 100,000 potential weekly visits, you are now serving 6 percent of this possible customer base. If you capture just 1 percent of the remaining possible visits, this means 940 additional transactions each week at $3.00 each. Additional sales, therefore, total $2,820 or a 16 percent increase in weekly sales volume.

If you can entice just one-half of your current customer base—3,000 people—back for one extra weekly visit at the same $3.00 average check, you boost sales volume by 50 percent.

Of course, the effect of any increase in transaction average will be multiplied if it is achieved in combination with either new customers or more frequent visits by current ones.

Naturally, the idea is to work constantly and consistently to achieve all of these goals, welding them into a reliable, unbeatable combination that will ensure the most business possible and will make the competition run and turn green with envy. If the true potential of the customer base in your trading area is thoroughly tapped, even major competitors will think twice about challenging you in a territory that is so decisively staked out as your own.

Neighborhood-restaurant marketing is the "great equalizer" among restaurants. Whether the restaurateur is an independent or chain-connected, or operates one store or more, it puts him or her on the same footing as any corporate giant in the trading area. It affects sales positively where they count— right at the cash register.

As you embrace neighborhood-restaurant marketing as the way of doing business, you can expect:

- Sustained customer loyalty
- Increased frequency of visits
- New customers
- Greater penetration of the trading area
- Higher checks
- Competitive edge
- Increased top-line sales and a filter effect to bottom-line sales
- Reinforcement of positive experience in the restaurant
- Motivated employees
- Reversal of negative sales trends

All of these add up to a stronger business. If you don't think it works, hop into your car at any time of day and drive to your local McDonald's or Burger King; then check out their nearby competition and your own restaurant. Then return to this book and learn how to put neighborhood-restaurant marketing to work for you.

A MENU
of successful
planning
techniques

IF you're starting to feel that I'd like to outfit you with a special pair of glasses that would only permit you to view your world as an arena for neighborhood-restaurant marketing, you're right. I realize that I'm asking you to make a habit of acting in a way that's unfamiliar to you. That's why I'm using these opening chapters to stress the basic tenets of neighborhood-restaurant marketing.

Underlying all successful neighborhood-restaurant marketing activities is disciplined planning. An experienced business person is always planning, even if he or she doesn't always call it that. Increasing prices to meet costs, scheduling employees' hours or one's own work, or anticipating a demand for a seasonal item and increasing the order for it—all these actions involve planning.

SEVEN KEYS TO PROFITABLE PLANNING

I have found that there are seven easy-to-turn planning keys that open the door to consistently higher retail sales. With these keys, you'll be able to open that door at will. Without them, that door will remain closed to you, permanently.

I have said that the seven keys are easy to turn, but this must be qualified. They are easy to turn only if you accept the fact that they must be turned in order and with disciplined and concentrated attention. In this chapter, I will briefly describe the keys to you. In the following chapters, I will show you how to use them.

Here's the key ring.

Key 1: Situation Analysis

How much do you really know about your business? Probably not as much as you should, or even as much as you think you do. Without a really thorough knowledge of your business you simply cannot undertake meaningful planning. Map out your sales trends. Find out who your customers are, where they come from, why and how often they visit the restaurant.

Are you really aware of what proportion of your profits comes from the various parts of your product mix? Are you properly staffed in regard to both quality and quantity? Is your staff properly motivated? How many of these questions could you answer concerning your competition?

These are the prime factors supporting sales and profits. They really determine, despite apparent year-end success, just how healthy your business is.

Key 2: Problems and Opportunities

Once the situation analysis is completed (in Chapter 3, you will be shown exactly how to do that), the results should be studied in terms of positive and negative facts that can be turned to your advantage through marketing.

For example, the situation analysis may make you firmly aware that the parking around the restaurant is really a problem. Access is blocked, possibly because of deliveries to the restaurant and to other businesses. Running an ad in a local paper announcing that parking tickets for a nearby garage will be validated or that small change will be offered for meter-feeding—with a minimum purchase—may turn the problem into an opportunity. Not only will regular customers be accommodated but new ones will be attracted as well. It's simr'e when you use neighborhood-restaurant marketing.

Beyond the immediate and practical identification of problems and opportunities is the necessity to probe deeper into the "whys" of the business. Are sales sagging on Saturdays when they should be peaking? That kind of a problem will be brought out by the situation analysis. Focusing directly on problems and opportunities will inform you about what's causing that sag and suggest what can be done about it.

Key 3: Objectives

Once the list of clearly defined marketing problems and opportunities is compiled, objectives can be set. Simply stated, an objective is a detailed statement of purpose.

The objectives being referred to here are marketing objectives: reasonable, practical, achievable, specific goals—with time limits—that can be reached through applied neighborhood-restaurant marketing. These can be measured, number against number, score against fumble, when the targeted time has elapsed.

Thus, one objective for a restaurant operation might read: "Increase net sales from the current weekly average of $10,000 to $11,000 by July 15, 1983." This objective is short, sweet, and to the point—but well thought out on the basis of the problems and opportunities isolated through the initial anaylsis.

Over the years, in imparting these principles to relative newcomers to disciplined planning, I've found that there are two things that are likely to confuse them somewhat. To reduce this possible confusion, it may be helpful to make two points:

1. Because the keys are so interrelated there is seeming repetition. It's intentional and necessary.
2. Because in daily life we're used to thinking from general ideas to particular ones, our minds stumble for a minute when we step from objectives (particular) to strategies (general) and back to tactics (particular) as we're about to do now.

Keep these points in mind—all will be well.

Key 4: Strategies

As previously indicated, strategies are general, broad, statements; they are intended to provide a framework for the overall actions taken to achieve objectives. Thus, combining the problem/opportunity and the objective we've mentioned before, a strategy statement might read: "Increase sales by attracting more customers who are likely to drive to the restaurant but are reluctant because they can't find parking."

Key 5: Tactics

A tactic is the actual promotional device used to execute your strategy and help meet your objective. Since we have a ready-made example of tactics, we'll use it: Running an ad in the local paper offering free parking with a minimum purchase. That's a particular tactic, chosen within the framework of your strategy and directed toward your objective. You may choose other tactics or even a set of tactics.

Key 6: Budget

For the purpose of this discussion, one brief and deceptively simple observation about budgeting promotions will be made: Funds allocated to marketing need not be huge, but they must be adequate. You will be taught how to apply that maxim throughout your marketing planning.

Key 7: Evaluation

A seat-of-the-pants, by-guess and by-golly attitude toward evaluation has been the kiss of death for many well-intentioned marketing programs.

Evaluation is far more than simply measuring results against objectives on the target date. A program must be monitored constantly with an eye to testing the validity of objectives, strategies, and tactics so that they may be revised according to their own soundness or to changing circumstances.

Evaluation is a two-part discipline. First, one must set up an evaluation routine and schedule and stick to them. Then, one must exercise mental toughness in accepting the conclusions and implications of the evaluation if they prove negative. If these directions are followed, the final sales-chart results should be extremely positive.

To use these Seven Keys on your own special door to success, they must be refined to fit its unique locks. This is done by determining the exact configuration of those locks, a task that can only be accomplished through research.

MARKET RESEARCH YOU CAN DO YOURSELF

Research, like marketing itself, has taken on a reputation of being costly and almost mysteriously complicated. This is nonsense. Market research is no more than the disciplined gathering, sorting and recording of facts and attitudes so that they can be interpreted for use in planning.

Most of the necessary data are as close as your restaurant. The balance are accessible within the three-to-five mile trading area. Further, the detailed guidance contained in this book should enable you and your staff to do all the necessary research, without resorting to outside help. However, because circumstances do vary, you will be guided on how to decide if hiring research consultants will work well in your case. You will also learn how to choose reliable consultants and how to derive maximum benefit from their service.

Before you begin to research for neighborhood-restaurant marketing—and particularly for Situation Analysis—it may be helpful to know that the information it requires falls into three general categories, according to how it can be compiled.

Category 1: Your Own Business Statistics

- Restaurant Characteristics
- Sales History and Information
- Transaction Counts
- Promotional History
- Average Purchase
- Product-Mix Trend

Category 2: Customer Demographics (ages, ethnic backgrounds, and family structures of customer base in the trading area)

- Customer Profile
- Visit Frequency
- Group Size
- Age Groupings

Category 3: Trading Area Background

- Traffic Generators (a place or activity where people congregate which has potential for generating increased sales by means of promotional incentive)
- Community Events
- Media Outlets
- Competitive Study

Much of the basic information required for Category 1 should be easily accessible from business records, although some searching, sorting, and simple calculation will have to be done. Other information can be garnered by sharpened observation or by reaching into your personal memory bank. In short, this research can be done in the restaurant, office, or den by referring to information and records already at hand.

The customer-related material in Category 2 also lends itself to in-restaurant research. But, it presents a particularly treacherous pitfall that you must be warned against: Many restaurateurs fail to grasp and use vital customer information because they take it for granted that they know far more about their customer base than they really do.

The origins of this hazardous situation are quite understandable. Because restaurateurs are in constant contact with their customers, they assume that they're accumulating useful knowledge about buying habits, age groupings, lifestyles, likes and dislikes. In fact, this assumption leads to that most "dangerous thing"—a little knowledge. Acting on that "little knowledge" alone can *cost you your business.*

By following the directions in this book, you can expand and upgrade your knowledge and thus plan your marketing so that *competitors will be deprived of their business.*

You must move from instinctive, informal, incidental observation of customer characteristics. Detailed customer-base information must be sought with disciplined consistency, and it must be recorded so that it can be easily retrieved and interpreted.

Category 3, the Trading Area Background Report, obviously moves the focal center of fact-gathering away from the store and into the residential and business sections within a three-to-five mile radius. Some field work must be done to amass information on important restaurant-traffic generators. Although personal observation is important, the Chamber of Commerce or local government unit can be of assistance.

The staff, who probably live within the trading area, may be able to give some insight on the traffic generators. Perhaps they have relatives working at a major traffic generator—a nearby office building, for instance—who can provide useful information.

The Chamber of Commerce should also be a good source for a roster of community events, although civic groups, churches, and schools should also be contacted to assure that the list is as complete as possible. The local librarian should be able to supplement your own familiarity with local media by directing you to proper source books.

At this point, it will be well worth your while to take a few minutes to skim through the first two chapters once again. They contain both the foundation and the framework for what will be discussed in the following chapters. As you reread them, please keep in mind that the cement for the foundation and rivets for the framework came from the same raw stuff—discipline. Without discipline there is no way to guarantee the strength of your marketing structure, and there is no discipline without commitment.

After you finish the review, you'll probably start feeling a need or, I hope, a hunger for more detailed information and instruction...which is just what is about to be served up.

eight critical guidelines for determining the real health of your restaurant

cHApTER THREE

This chapter will discuss precisely how to turn the first of the Seven Keys, Situation Analysis (S/A). The chapter contains a comprehensive series of worksheets to be completed. There are eight sets of worksheets, each prefaced by a page that introduces a specific S/A element and a statement of its primary purposes.

However, you *should not* pick up a pencil and start randomly filling in the blanks on the sheets. You should read through all the prefaces and sheets carefully, keeping in mind the basic research suggestions made in Chapter 2. You should also read these sheets with an awareness that a sound S/A is absolutely critical to the mastery of neighborhood-restaurant marketing. *You can't succeed without one!*

The validity of the problems and opportunities identified, the objectives set, and the strategies and tactics chosen are directly proportional to the thoroughness and accuracy of analysis. Honesty in rating yourself and your competition is equally important.

Here we go!

STEP 1: RESTAURANT
BACKGROUND INFORMATION

This one-sheet general record will be helpful in terms of allow-ing you to focus directly on the physical, locational aspects of the business that could positively or negatively affect the type of marketing activities you implement. Also, should you want to ask advice from an outside source, this chart, along with the others, will be extremely important in bringing them up to date about the business.

Be sure to complete as thoroughly as possible the section regarding marketing factors. For example, if your restaurant has high pedestrian traffic, as in a downtown situation, you may want to distribute flyers with a special offer. If the restau-rant sign isn't visible enough, you may consider getting another sign.

*The worksheets are intended as master copies to be expanded and duplicated.

Figure 3.1   Restaurant Background Information

DATE COMPILED _____
by _____

RESTAURANT BACKGROUND INFORMATION

General Information

1. Restaurant name _____
2. Address _____
3. Phone _____
4. Manager's name _____
5. Restaurant opening date _____
6. Number of registers _____
7. Parking spaces _____
8. Number of seats if applicable _____
9. _____
10. _____

Marketing Factors

List any physical characteristics that could affect marketing either positively or negatively.

1. _____

2. _____

3. _____

4. _____

5. _____

6. _____

7. _____

8. _____

9. _____

10. _____

STEP 2: SALES AND TRANSACTION
COUNT ANALYSIS

Enter monthly sales and transaction counts from last year and this year. Record the actual percent change where indicated. Also take into consideration seasonal trends, weather factors, and price increases. This vital information will allow you to spot sales trends, whether favorable or unfavorable, and to plan appropriate marketing action.

Remember that the only true growth indicators are transaction counts since they factor out inflation, which would be reflected in your monthly sales. If you have two consecutive months in which your comparable sales and/or transaction counts are lower than the same time period last year, then immediate marketing activity may be indicated.

Figure 3.2 Sales and Transaction Count Analysis

MONTHLY SALES AND TRANSACTION COUNT ANALYSIS

Monthly Sales				Monthly Trans. Count			
Month	1982	1983	% Change	Month	1982	1983	% Change
Jan.				Jan.			
Feb.				Feb.			
Mar.				Mar.			
April				April			
May				May			
June				June			
July				July			
Aug.				Aug.			
Sept.				Sept.			
Oct.				Oct.			
Nov.				Nov.			
Dec.				Dec.			
TOTALS				TOTALS			

STEP 3: TRANSACTION COUNT, AVERAGE CHECK BY DAY PART

To further isolate and identify specific sales period problems and opportunities, you must plot at least twelve weeks of transaction counts and average checks by day part and day of week. The standard day parts are open–2PM, 2PM–5PM, 5PM–8PM, and 8PM–close. If your restaurant does a significant breakfast business you may wish to add another day part: open–11AM.

Once this is completed, analyze the information to determine which day and day parts are making the most and the least contributions to the overall sales picture.

For example, if Wednesday night dinners are unusually high compared to the rest of the weekday dinner business try to find out why. Is it due to heavy shopping traffic or is a nearby factory perhaps running a night shift, prompting employees to take their dinner breaks at your restaurant? Both of these situations could represent significant promotional opportunities once they are recognized.

Conversely, if evening business is trending down several nights a week for no apparent reason, this could indicate the need for special marketing emphasis for that day part. Also consider other factors, like changes in the average check from one day part to another. If there is a significant drop, maybe the staff could use some instruction in suggestive selling or maybe the schedule should be changed.

Figure 3.3 Transaction Count, Average Check by Day Part

TRANSACTION COUNT
AVERAGE CHECK BY DAY PART

		Sunday		Monday		Tuesday		Wednesday		Thursday		Friday		Saturday	
		T.C.	Avg. Ck.	T.C.	Avg. Ck.	T.C.	Avg. Ck.	T.C.	Avg. Ck.	T.C.	Avg. Ck.	T.C.	Avg. Ck.	T.C.	Avg. Ck.
Week 1	1.														
	2.														
	3.														
	4.														
Week 2	1.														
	2.														
	3.														
	4.														
Week 3	1.														
	2.														
	3.														
	4.														
Week 4	1.														
	2.														
	3.														
	4.														
Week 5	1.														
	2.														
	3.														
	4.														
Week 6	1.														
	2.														
	2.														
	4.														
TOTAL															

1 = Open–2 PM; 2 = 2 PM–5 PM; 3 = 5 PM–8 PM; 4 = 8 PM–Close.

STEP 4: PRIMARY COMPETITIVE ANALYSIS

In order to maintain and increase your share of the business you must be aware of how your major competitors stack up. For each primary competitor, complete the information as accurately as possible, including their estimated volume, major marketing activities, operational strengths and weaknesses, their products and pricing strategy, and any other factors that could impact on your business either positively or negatively.

After the chart is completed, compare each competitor's strengths and weaknesses to your own. Through this process you will be able to ascertain where competitive inroads can be made into your business and where to take appropriate action. You'll be able to isolate competitive weaknesses and turn them into promotional opportunities.

When studying the competition, always look for their U.S.P. (Unique Selling Proposition). That's the product, service, or customer appeal that sets them apart. It's important to decide if their U.S.P. is truly a meaningful competitive factor when compared to your own U.S.P.

Figure 3.4 Primary Competitive Analysis

PRIMARY COMPETITIVE ANALYSIS

	Competitor I	Competitor II	Competitor III	Competitor IV	Competitor V
Name					
Proximity					
Est. Volume					
Mktg. Activities– List Past 12 Mo. Programs					
	1)	1)	1)	1)	1)
	2)	2)	2)	2)	2)
	3)	3)	3)	3)	3)
	4)	4)	4)	4)	4)
Operations					
List Strengths and Weaknesses					
	1)	1)	1)	1)	1)
	2)	2)	2)	2)	2)
	3)	3)	3)	3)	3)
	4)	4)	4)	4)	4)
	5)	5)	5)	5)	5)
Product Pricing– List Major Products and Prices					
	1) ____ 4) ____	1) ____ 4) ____	1) ____ 4) ____	1) ____ 4) ____	1) ____ 4) ____
	2) ____ 5) ____	2) ____ 5) ____	2) ____ 5) ____	2) ____ 5) ____	2) ____ 5) ____
	3) ____ 6) ____	3) ____ 6) ____	3) ____ 6) ____	3) ____ 6) ____	3) ____ 6) ____
Comments					

STEP 5: TRADING AREA PROFILE

These charts will provide you with pertinent information regarding the customer demographics of your trading area, along with traffic generator opportunities. Customer demographics are the ages, ethnic backgrounds, and family structures of your customers as well as of the surrounding population in the trading area. A traffic generator is any place or activity where people congregate that, through promotional incentive, has the potential for generating increased sales for your restaurant. These are places such as retailers, schools, churches, office buildings, etc.

Complete the charts as accurately as possible from your own knowledge and observation of your business and trading area. You may contact your local Chamber of Commerce or utilize the most recent census information available at your local library for assistance in completing the demographic portion of the study.

Once the study is completed, match up your prime demographic target with the appropriate types of traffic generators for promotional purposes. For example, if your target market is eighteen to thirty-four years of age and family oriented, then you might investigate tying in promotionally with a local department store or a movie theatre showing a family type film.

Remember your restaurant customer traffic should reflect the demographic patterns of the surrounding trading area to afford the greatest potential for increasing your business. If your restaurant is geared toward attracting single adults, aged nineteen to twenty-four, but the greatest concentration of population falls within the eighteen to thirty-four range, it might be advisable to re-position your restaurant concept to capitalize on the larger potential customer base, in the eighteen to thirty-four age range.

Figure 3.5　Traffic Generator Summary

TRAFFIC GENERATOR SUMMARY

RETAIL	Name	Type of Merchandise	# of Employees	Contact
1)				
2)				
3)				
4)				
5)				
6)				

SCHOOLS	Name	Type	# of Students	Contact
1)				
2)				
3)				
4)				
5)				

OFFICE/ INDUSTRIAL	Name	Type	# of Employees	Contact
1)				
2)				
3)				
4)				

RELIGIOUS	Name	Type	Size of Congregation	Contact
1)				
2)				
3)				

RECREATION	Name	Type	# of Participants	Contact
1)				
2)				

MISCELLANEOUS	Name	Type	Size/#	Contact
1)				
2)				

PRIME TRADING AREA ANALYSIS

Trading Area (3-5 Mile Radius or 10-Minute Driving Time)

1. Ethnic Breakout

    a. Caucasian _____%

    b. Black _____%

    c. Hispanic _____%

    d. Other _____%

2. Trading Area Demographics

    a. Under 18 _____%

    b. 19-24 _____%

    c. 25-34 _____%

    d. 35-49 _____%

    e. 49 plus _____%

Restaurant Traffic

1. Ethnic Breakout

    a. Caucasian _____%

    b. Black _____%

    c. Hispanic _____%

    d. Other _____%

Figure 3.6 Trading Area Analysis

TRADING AREA ANALYSIS (continued)

Restaurant Traffic (continued)

2. **Customer Demographics**

   a. Under 18 _____%

   b. 19-24 _____%

   c. 25-34 _____%

   d. 35-49 _____%

   e. 49 plus _____%

3. **Day Part Analysis Percentage**

   a. Breakfast (open - 11 a.m.) _____%

   b. Lunch (11 a.m. - 2 p.m.) _____%

   c. Afternoon (2 - 5 p.m.) _____%

   d. Dinner (5 - 8 p.m.) _____%

   e. Night (8 - close) _____%

4. **Restaurant Traffic Percentage**

   a. Living in trading area _____%

   b. Working in trading area _____%

   c. Transient _____%

5. **Group Sizes**

   a. 3 or more _____%

   b. 2 _____%

   c. 1 _____%

STEP 6: COMMUNITY EVENTS

Worthwhile participation in selected community events is an excellent way to build and maintain increased neighborhood visibility and enhance customer loyalty. The key to taking greatest advantage of these opportunities is to plan in advance.

List all the community events as far in advance as possible and decide if you would like to participate. Note the type of event, the organization involved, and the person to contact; and be sure to allow enough time for proper promotional planning. Include activities such as parades, fund raising activities, church bazaars, school events, etc.

Also keep a record of all those who call on you for donations or community projects. Note if you participated and if you wish to participate again. These can be valuable contacts for many sales-building and public relations programs.

Figure 3.7 Community Events

COMMUNITY EVENTS

Month	Name of Organization	Type of Event	Participate Yes	No	Contact
January	1.) _____ 2.) _____				
February	1.) _____ 2.) _____ 3.) _____				
March	1.) _____ 2.) _____ 3.) _____				
April	1.) _____ 2.) _____ 3.) _____				
May	1.) _____ 2.) _____				
June	1.) _____ 2.) _____ 3.) _____				
July	1.) _____ 2.) _____				
August	1.) _____ 2.) _____				
September	1.) _____ 2.) _____ 3.) _____				
October	1.) _____ 2.) _____ 3.) _____				
November	1.) _____ 2.) _____ 3.) _____				
December	1.) _____ 2.) _____				

STEP 7: LOCAL MEDIA AND
NEWSMAKER INFORMATION

List relevant information about local advertising vehicles. Be aware of the cost, placement guidelines, and publication information regarding local newspapers in your community. Know spot cost and formats of any local radio stations along with poster costs of any billboard companies. Try to develop local media contacts as well, such as editors of newspapers and radio D.J.'s. These contacts will be useful to you when the opportunity arises for generating publicity for a promotion.

Getting free media attention is no easy task; but keep in mind that the more innovative or worthwhile your promotion, the better the chance of obtaining media coverage.

Also keep a record of well-known personalities in your community, such as politicians, sports figures, and community leaders. Occasionally you may have the opportunity to include one of these newsmakers in your promotions, thus enhancing your chances of getting media coverage for the event. For example, have a community leader participate in a check presentation to a charitable organization.

Figure 3.8 Local Media and Newsmaker Information

LOCAL MEDIA AND NEWSMAKER INFORMATION

Advertising/ Publicity					Local Newsmakers

Radio

$ Spot Rate

Station	60 sec.	30 sec.	Format	Contact
1)				
2)				
3)				

Newspaper

Name	Rate	Daily/Weekly	Contact
1)			
2)			
3)			
4)			
5)			

Billboard

Name	Poster Cost	Contact
1)		
2)		

Comments:

Local Newsmakers

1)

2)

3)

4)

5)

6)

7)

8)

STEP 8: RESTAURANT MARKETING HISTORY

It's important to evaluate the results of every marketing activity implemented. This is the only way to determine if the program achieved the desired goals and was profitable and cost efficient. By keeping accurate records you'll be able to determine if the program has repeat value. It's impossible to remember the effects of every program that is implemented; so, if you take the time to complete this chart, you will have a valuable tool for future promotional and budgetary planning. It will certainly help prevent the wasteful allocation of promotional dollars.

Figure 3.9 Restaurant Marketing History

RESTAURANT MARKETING HISTORY

Marketing Program	Dates Used	Type of Advertising	In-Restaurant Merchandising Materials	Total Cost	Evaluation
1)	from ____ to ____				
2)	from ____ to ____				
3)	from ____ to ____				
4)	from ____ to ____				
5)	from ____ to ____				
6)	from ____ to ____				

USING THE WORKSHEETS

As you read through your worksheets, you will see why you shouldn't attempt to fill in random statistics and facts. The approach should be far more disciplined. In fact, you may feel that you have quite a bit of work cut out for you. Don't be discouraged. It can be done. Others have done it. Neighborhood-restaurant marketing *is* worth the effort. But, you do have to be committed to it.

I could attempt to reassure you by pointing out that the tasks covered in this chapter make up the bulk of basic marketing planning and that future steps will become easier for it. This is all true. However, I must also acknowledge that we've reached a point where a decision must be made. You could go on reading the rest of this book and you would probably pick up enough information to improve your marketing and promotion activities. But, if you really want to succeed, now is the time for deciding that it's worth some hard work.

The worksheets are intended as master copies for duplication, to enable you to analyze more than one restaurant, if that is pertinent to your operations. It will also enable you to hand out copies to those staff members who may be helpful in supplying needed information.

There are a number of things to be considered in making these fact-gathering assignments. Although it is good to make use of employee slack time—getting a bonus in staff productivity, you should avoid creating the impression of setting up make-work projects. However, the assignments should also not be constantly sloughed off in favor of routine. Allow reasonable time, but set deadlines and see that they are met.

Regard these initial neighborhood-restaurant marketing efforts as an opportunity to acquaint the whole staff with your plans to structure a sales-building marketing program and to enlist their enthusiasm in pursuing the future promotional activities it will entail. Try to accomplish this even if the staffing situation or other factors indicate that it might be most practical to either undertake the task yourself, assign the job to one staff member, or—a course to be discouraged for cost reasons—temporarily hire outside assistance.

The finished worksheets will give you a broader and deeper understanding of and familiarity with the business and with the major marketing factors affecting it. Studying these sheets for trends and for previously buried facts and attitudes will raise your level of market awareness to new heights. Most important, you will have been prepared for the climb to a still higher vantage point from which to exercise a restaurant-oriented view of marketing.

RESEARCH

To obtain an even clearer view of marketing possibilities, you should complete and confirm your Situation Analysis with more concentrated consumer research. This research will serve two basic purposes. First, it will confirm—or creatively challenge—the information already recorded about your customer base. Second, it will probe more deeply into the make-up of the base to unearth still more opportunities for exploiting and expanding it.

Some of the specific customer and sales information to confirm or uncover would answer these questions:

- What are the real strengths and weaknesses of the trading area?
- Is the current penetration of that area adequate? Where and how does it fall short?
- How often do current customers visit the restaurant?
- How often do customers visit the competition?
- Where do customers come from before visiting the restaurant? Home? Office? Bank? Shopping malls?
- Do customers come alone or in groups?
- Where do they go when they leave?
- How do customers rate the restaurant in comparison to competitors?
- What age groups predominate in the customer mix?

If you do *not* feel confident of the depth or validity of your answers to these questions, you should conduct appropriate research. Two broad types of research are used to obtain accurate answers to these retailing questions: in-store research and out-of-store research.

In-Store Research

This is an approach that is in wide use. In-store research is an extremely economical and effective way to obtain information about the current customer base that can later be used in market planning. As it is likely that you will be conducting in-store research, detailed instructions and a sample questionnaire follow.

The Sample Size/When to Interview. Ideally, you should plan to survey between 500 and 800 customers to obtain a sufficient sample size. The size of the total sample should be equally divided over a typical 4-day period which represents all facets of your customer traffic. For example, by interviewing your customers from Thursday to Sunday, weekday and weekend business will be accounted for, along with other important changes in customer base, such as group size, frequency, and average check.

Interviews should be conducted from opening to closing because it's important to achieve a representation of your customer base spread over all hours of operation. This is extremely important since the characteristics of your customer base are likely to vary depending on the time of day interviewed. You certainly wouldn't want to develop a marketing plan based on only a portion of your customers' opinions and patterns.

Hourly interview quotas should be established. The quotas should be set up so that the number of customers interviewed per hour is equal to the percent of sales that hour represents from the total day's sales. For example, assume you are going to interview a total of 800 customers from Thursday to Sunday, so 200 interviews must be completed each day. As the chart illustrates, each day's sales should be expressed on an hourly basis as a percentage of total sales for that day:

Thursday Sales	Hourly Sales as Percentage of Total	Number of Interviews Per Hour
Open-11am	5%	10
11-12pm	5%	10
1-2pm	10%	20
2-3pm	3%	6
3-4pm	4%	8
4-5pm	10%	20
5-6pm	14%	28
6-7pm	20%	40
7-8pm	10%	20
8-9pm	4%	8
9-10pm	6%	12
10-Close	9%	18
Total	100%	Total 200

This guideline will guarantee a representative customer base sample.

How the Interviewer Should Dress. Interviewers should not wear any restaurant uniforms or identification; street clothes are recommended. The image projected to the customers should be one of impartiality, as this will not intimidate them in case they have any negative comments to make, which you certainly would want to be aware of.

How to Approach a Customer. Interviewers should not approach the customer with a yes or no question such as, "Excuse me, do you have a few minutes to answer some questions?" when asking for the interview. This type of question forces the customer to think about all the reasons why they don't have the time or desire to participate in the survey. Instead, start with a positive statement like, "Excuse me, Sir (or Miss), (INSERT

RESTAURANT NAME) is conducting a survey to learn how to serve you better." Then ask the first question. By not giving people the option of answering "*No*" to being interviewed, you will achieve a much higher success rate of completing the hourly interview quotas.

The Length of the Interview. Don't make the interview too lengthy, or people will terminate the interview and you'll be left with an incomplete questionnaire.

The following questionnaire has 16 questions. With practice, your employees should be able to complete one interview in five minutes, which is acceptable. Obviously use your judgment; if you're getting a high number of uncompleted interviews, then it may be necessary to reduce the number of questions.

Constructing the Questionnaire. Review the survey questions provided as a guide for building a questionnaire. Use all the questions or a portion of them. Use your specific knowledge of your restaurant to formulate a questionnaire most suited to your individual needs.

IN-STORE SURVEY QUESTIONNAIRE

---

1. Where were you *before* coming to this (INSERT RESTAURANT NAME)?

    Home ☐   Work ☐   Shopping ☐   School ☐
    Other ☐

2. Where do you plan to go after leaving the restaurant?

    Home ☐   Work ☐   Shopping ☐   School ☐
    Other ☐

3. Including today's visit, how many times have you been to (INSERT RESTAURANT'S NAME) in the last month?

   1st visit ☐   1 Time ☐   2-4 Times ☐   5 or more ☐

4. What meal did you have at (INSERT RESTAURANT NAME) today?

   Breakfast ☐   Lunch ☐   Dinner ☐

   Afternoon Snack ☐   Evening Snack ☐

5. Today is what day of the week?

   Mon-Thurs ☐   Friday ☐   Saturday ☐   Sunday ☐

6. Have you ever eaten in (INSERT RESTAURANT NAME)?

   Yes ☐   No ☐   If yes, how often? _____

7. Will you be eating in ☐   or taking out ☐   today's purchase?

8. How many people are with you or did you order for?

   None ☐   One ☐   Two ☐   Three ☐   Four ☐

   5 or more ☐

9. How many people are in your household?

   One ☐   Two ☐   Three ☐   Four ☐   5 or more ☐

10. Which of the following age groups most clearly represents your age?

    15-19 ☐   20-24 ☐   25-29 ☐

    30-39 ☐   40-49 ☐   50+ ☐

11. How much did you spend today? $_____

12. How long does it take you to drive or walk from your house or apartment to (INSERT RESTAURANT NAME)?
    Under 5 min ☐   6-10 ☐   11-15 min ☐   16-25 ☐
    25+ min ☐

13. What other (INSERT MAJOR PROJECT CATEGORY) restaurants have you visited in the past month?
    _____

    _____

14. How often have you visited there in the past month?
    _____

15. If you have already tried (INSERT RESTAURANT NAME), how do you rate it compared to the competition in these categories?

    (INSERT YOUR
    MAJOR PRODUCT):   Much better   ____
                        Better   ____
                        Satisfactory   ____
                        Worse   ____
                        Same   ____

    CLEANLINESS: Much better   ____
                        Better   ____
                        Satisfactory   ____
                        Worse   ____
                        Same   ____

    SERVICE: Much better   ____
                        Better   ____
                        Satisfactory   ____
                        Worse   ____
                        Same   ____

PRICE VALUE: Much better   ——
                        Better   ——
                        Satisfactory ——
                        Worse   ——
                        Same   ——

16. List in order your three favorite radio stations.

      _____

      _____

      _____

17. Thanks for answering these questions. We'll analyze them carefully. The results will tell us how we can be of better service to you.

     (Interviewer's closing remarks.)

Out-of-Store Research

The focus of this type of research is not on current customers but on the population-at-large in the trading area. Its purpose is to measure market potential as well as general consumer attitudes and trends regarding goods or services.

This is normally accomplished efficiently through telephone interviews of a random population sample simply drawn from phone company directories. For more information, you should seek assistance from a local research company. Another workable approach is to station interviewers at busy mall or community locations to randomly question passers-by.

Least advisable of all common out-of-store research techniques is direct-mail queries. This approach has become somewhat popular because of the success of direct-mail sales. Don't be misled! Direct mail questionnaires are costly and low response rates (which are usually the case) render their results almost totally useless.

PERSONAL VERSUS PROFESSIONAL RESEARCH

These fundamental techniques, for the most part, lend themselves to common-sense definition of the questions to be answered, simple questionnaire design, ease of execution, and practical interpretation. They can be more than adequately carried out by the restaurateur or staff members.

Take, for instance, an in-store survey. You know what you want to find out, so you adapt the sample questionnaire to find pertinent answers. You should be able to rely on your staff for courteous and thorough interviewing and on your own business experience for meaningful interpretation.

However, because of staffing restrictions or the complexity of your particular business, you may feel that you wish to seek outside professional help. If this is the case, remember that you should be able to find a reliable firm that will help you with just certain aspects of your research or one that will provide guidance to your own efforts. Don't let a firm take on the whole assignment at higher cost.

Common business sense also comes into play in choosing a research firm. You should have solid answers to the following questions:

1. How long has the firm been in business? Can they refer you to other clients?
2. Who of the firm's principals and staff will be assigned to your restaurant? Do they have enough experience in the restaurant business to be truly helpful?
3. Does the firm's proposal indicate an accurate understanding of your research aims? Does it contain costly "bells and whistles" or candid, down-to-earth approaches?
4. Is the firm's timetable reasonable?
5. Are its costs reasonable?
6. Are you *sure* you can't do it yourself?

The last question is not intended as a negative reflection on the integrity of research firms. It is simply true that most of the retailing research needed for neighborhood-restaurant marketing can be competently performed by you and your staff. Although you shouldn't stint unnecessarily, remember the budgeting maxim previously stated: Marketing budgets need not be huge but they must be adequate. What is saved on research now can be allocated to promotion later.

On to problems and opportunities. . .

HOW TO
SELECT—
AND HIT—
TARGETS OF
OPPORTUNITY

chapter four

Now that you've completed work on your Situation Analysis you are ready to put its results to work.

A great deal of data has been amassed about your business. You should now allot some definite periods of time over the next several days to sift through this information. Read through each finished work sheet and research report as carefully as you read your financial statements. Regard your S/A documents as photo negatives. Your careful study of them will develop them into a more sharply focused picture of the business and the market than you've ever had before.

PROBLEMS AND OPPORTUNITIES AS BASES FOR OBJECTIVES

First read over all the material so that you can begin to absorb it. Then, take each section of the S/A separately and read it with the intention of identifying particular problems and opportunities. And remember that you are looking for problems and opportunities that will respond to *marketing action*.

You might find, as in our example of parking difficulties, that a problem may itself present an opportunity. In most cases, however, you will isolate problems and opportunities that do not have such a clear-cut relationship. So don't expect such convenient match-ups between the two categories.

Refer to Figure 4.1 for an example of how problems and opportunities are most likely to emerge from the study of an S/A. Use copies of the blank problem and opportunity sheet (Figure 4.2) to list *all* the problems and opportunities you can find. Give as much pertinent detail as possible. Don't trust your memory, but don't swamp yourself with words. Then give the S/A material one more careful reading. This will fix the data more firmly in your mind and may result in further identification of problems and opportunities.

After you are sure that you've thought of all possible marketing-related problems and opportunities in your situation and have listed them, start to rank them in order of priority. Assign priority according to these two criteria:

1. *Urgency* (How serious is the problem? How outstanding is the opportunity?)
2. *Achievability* (Can the problem be attacked or the opportunity be developed through reasonable and economical marketing efforts?)

PROBLEMS	OPPORTUNITIES
• Average check delined from $2.70 to $1.50 • Total sales declining over past three months • Customer count 3% down compared to year before • New competition opened up three blocks west four months ago—good quality products and service at competitive prices • Inadequate customer parking	• Large residential/family base population • Significant number of traffic generators including hospitals, factories, retail shopping center, three high schools, one college, six restaurants • Community Event coming up—Hospital Charity Bazaar • New product introduction in two months

Figure 4.1

PROBLEMS   **OPPORTUNITIES**

Figure 4.2

Once you've ranked your problems and opportunities through realistic application of these criteria, choose the top three or four as your immediate areas of action. Don't bite off more than you can chew. Most of the items at the bottom of your list can either wait for future action or eventually may be discarded altogether.

DEFINING OBJECTIVES

Now you are in possession of the second key and ready to start fashioning the third for yourself. You will recall that in Chapter Two we briefly discussed the third key, Objectives. Objectives were defined as practical, specific targets to be reached within set time limits; and your success or failure in meeting them was unmistakably measurable in hard numbers. That description will now be elaborated.

First, you should base your objectives on the problems or opportunities you have identified. The purpose of identifying problems and opportunities was to provide you with the raw material that objectives are made of. But you must treat this raw material with care before it can become useful.

For instance, a common problem is declining sales, and it may be tempting to simply construct an objective that would call for an overall 2 percent increase in gross sales by the end of the next six months. On the face of it, that might seem a useful, even laudable, objective. But closer examination might well reveal that such an objective is not truly *meaningful* in terms of bottom-line profitability. The marketing effort it would require could use up all the profit margin you might hope to build. That 2 percent increase could be a target not worth the ammunition. So, *don't set your sights too low*. If an objective is too easily attainable, it is probably not worth pursuing. You have got to be tough on yourself.

It is important, however, that you are not *too* tough on yourself. Your objective has to be *achievable* in terms of available resources. Your own common sense would naturally prevent you from charging wildly toward an obviously extreme sales increase of, say, 100 percent over six months. However, enthusiasm and ambition could still lure you into setting objectives that would uselessly stretch your resources and energies.

There is a related trap you should avoid: setting targets that you know are unreasonable (figuring that even a shortfall will leave you ahead of the game). It just doesn't work out. Overcommitment of resources diverts you from putting the proper amount of effort into doing something effective for your business.

Your best guide to setting achievable goals is the new knowledge that you gained about your business through your S/A. Reading beyond the figures that show the sales decline you are trying to overcome will give you a workable idea of the capacity of your restaurant to build volume.

In addition to being meaningful and achievable, your objectives should be measurable. You build in a prime element of measurability when you include a time limit. When that time has elapsed, you will be ready to evaluate the results of your efforts.

Setting an objective in concrete terms—an increased percentage of customer visit frequency, a percentage rise in gross sales, a larger dollar amount per average purchase—will make results easily measurable. But don't take the measurement for granted. Check it out. It's the only way you'll know if your programs are working and if you are getting a return on your marketing dollar and investment.

Although all of the seven keys are interrelated, there is a particularly close relationship among objectives, strategies, and tactics. In fact, they are inseparable, as you will see in the following pages.

Once the objective is clearly stated, you must formulate your plan for achieving it. That plan is your strategy. The strategy may partially repeat the objective but it will invariably extend it, stating a general action to be taken and a customer grouping against which that action will be targeted. This can best be illustrated by the following examples:

1. *Objective:* To increase average customer purchase by $2.00 by June 30, 19—.
   Strategy: Appeal to primary target audience (18-49) with value-oriented promotions.

2. *Objective:* To increase customer visits by two times a month by June 30, 19—.
   Strategy: Run continuity promotions directed at the existing customer base.

3. *Objective:* To increase afternoon traffic (1 PM-4 PM) by 15% by June 30, 19—.
   Strategy: Together with local merchants, implement joint promotions geared toward women in the trading area.

Although only one strategy has been listed for each objective, any given objective may be addressed by several strategies. For instance, the overall objective, "Increase total annual sales by 10 percent, effective June 30, 19—," could be supported by all of the strategies shown.

Tactics, in marketing, are the individual promotional activities you choose to actualize your strategies. Tactics involve contact between your store and your target marketing groups. Newspaper ads, in-store promotions, radio time, and personal appearances by celebrities are all tactics. Let's expand upon the objective/strategy illustration by adding appropriate tactics:

1. *Objective:* To increase average customer purchase by $2.00 by June 30, 19—.
   Strategy: Appeal to primary target audience (18-49) with value-oriented promotions.
   Tactic: Create package discount offers. For example, buy two sandwiches at the regular price and receive one free.

2. *Objective:* To increase customer visits by two times a month by June 30, 19—.

Strategy: Run continuity promotions directed at the existing customer base.

Tactic: Distribute bonus coupons to existing customers offering a special discount on their next visit.

3. *Objective:* To increase afternoon traffic (1 PM-4 PM) by 15% by June 30, 19—.

Strategy: Together with local merchants, implement joint promotions geared toward women in the trading area.

Tactic: Set up cross promotions. For example, when a customer presents a register receipt from a cooperating retailer, he or she receives a special value at your restaurant.

Subsequent chapters will follow on specific tactics and will discuss how to make the most of them in your particular situation. For now, here is a general rule regarding tactics: When planning tactics, *always* consider seasonal trends, weather probability, special events, and holidays. To extract maximum advantage from promotions tie your promotions in with other activities, avoid possible conflicts with community activities, and carefully schedule promotions to avoid probable bad weather.

HOW TO BUDGET NEIGHBORHOOD-RESTAURANT MARKETING

The most important thing that can be said about budgeting is: *Do it!* A detailed budget, projected over a year, is essential to proper neighborhood-restaurant marketing planning. Marketing is a year-long activity. To provide adequate funds you must plan that far ahead. Do not waste your money by merely allocating it randomly to pay for executing particular tactics. I can assure you that this is just like throwing away thirty-three cents out of every promotional dollar.

Here are some questions you should answer before you plan your neighborhood-restaurant marketing budget:

1. Are you part of a larger chain and already contributing to an overall advertising budget? How can neighborhood-restaurant marketing supplement that advertising most economically?
2. How aggressive is your competition?
3. What word and situation best describes your restaurant's business:
   a. *Pioneer*—new, recently opened enterprise
   b. *Competitive*—struggling for your market share
   c. *Retentive*—well-established in your community?
4. Is your restaurant's financial condition strong or weak?

Accurate answers to these questions will help you determine what percentage of your gross sales should be allocated to neighborhood-restaurant marketing.

When constructing a budget, there are three basic approaches: (1) fit the budget to the job; (2) fit the job to the budget; and (3) combine numbers 1 and 2.

If you choose method one, start by preparing a promotional calendar (see Figure 4.3). State what you would really like to do to fulfill your strategies and reach your objectives, and initially ignore costs. Then, go back over this ideal plan and cost out each tactic you have selected, arriving at a total cost for the plan.

There are three general elements in tactic costing:

1. *Media Expense:* money paid to buy newspaper space and radio time or to rent billboards.
2. *Production Expense:* money paid for the creative and physical production of newspaper ads, billboard posters, or radio commercials. This might also include direct mail preparation and postage and design and printing of point-of-purchase materials such as restaurant tray liners, coupons, posters, or banners.
3. *Promotional Expense:* money paid as fees for celebrity personal appearances, as contest prizes, or for advertising specialties such as imprinted glasses, T-shirts, balloons, or frisbees.

Each tactic should be broken down according to the applicable expense categories. For tactic costing, do not include the cost of employee time or the cost of your own time; you should be able to figure these as ordinary business assignments.

Once you have arrived at the total cost of your ideal twelve-month marketing plan, project your monthly sales for the same period. Then calculate what percentage of the sales total your ideal plan will cost. If this figure exceeds 5 percent, you should start cutting back on some of the excess to arrive at a realistic expenditure. If the planned promotional expenditure is substantially less than 2 percent of sales, you should review the program to see if you've skimped unnecessarily and damaged your prospects of marketing success.

Don't be concerned that your monthly sales totals are projections. As you track your sales regularly, you can revise the plan costs as necessary. At least you will be working within a well-thought-out framework.

The second method, fitting the plan to the budget, involves allocating an arbitrary monthly percentage of gross sales to promotion, projecting sales, and figuring out what can be spent each month. Then you can plan tactics that fit your budget.

The third approach to budgeting for neighborhood-restaurant marketing combines the first two and often proves most effective for smaller restaurant operations.

Project your twelve-month sales and calculate a total marketing budget that you feel comfortable with. Then, separately construct and cost out a twelve-month marketing tactic schedule that you feel will best implement your strategies and attain your objectives. Use your judgment in reconciling discrepancies between the two resulting figures. Your purpose is to determine what will do the job.

There are four things to remember when you tackle a promotion budget. First, you are planning an investment, not just an expenditure. Second, although you can't expect a direct payback on each tactic you choose, each tactic creates continuity and momentum as part of a total program. Third, a budget is a necessity. And fourth, a budget need not be huge, but it must be adequate.

19— MARKETING BUDGET PLANNING GUIDE

	Last Year's Sales	Last Year's Advertising %	This Year's Projected Sales	This Year's Projected Advertising %	Advertising Costs	This Year's Actual Sales	Actual Advertising Cost
January							
February							
March							
April							
May							
June							
July							
August							
September							
October							
November							
December							
Total							

Figure 4.3 Budget Planning Guide

MEASURING THE RETURN ON YOUR MARKETING INVESTMENT

EXCITEMENT, enthusiasm, and anticipation often contribute to the effective structuring of a marketing plan. For some reason though, the force of these attitudes seems to weaken dramatically when it comes to turning the seventh key—evaluation. Perhaps this is because evaluation puts judgment and ego on the line in a way that many people defensively resist. It may also be that the mechanics of disciplined evaluation seem so tedious that people tend to fall back on the usual year-end review of sales to measure the success of promotional programs. Perhaps the anxiety to start promotions causes an instinctive rebellion against taking the time needed to set up proper evaluation procedures.

Neighborhood-restaurant marketing demands realistic, painstaking, and immediate evaluation of *each* promotional activity. Moreover, the methods of evaluation should be understood and put into place *before* a promotion is undertaken.

Evaluation should be aimed at answering three basic questions:

1. Did the promotion reach its stated objective?
2. Was the promotion cost-efficient?
3. Should the promotion be repeated, modified, or scrapped?

These questions and their answers are obviously interrelated. The results must be balanced against cost-efficiency, not only to determine past success but to gain the experience and insight that will make you an increasingly successful marketer for your own business.

THE EVALUATION PROCESS: PROOF OF THE PUDDING

Meaningful evaluation is divided into a series of three general calculations:

1. Pre-promotional Payout
2. Promotional Appraisal
3. Post-promotional Payout

Let's examine how these calculations would be performed for a hypothetical promotion at a submarine sandwich restaurant.

   This first calculation is intended to *project* the *profitability* of a given promotion. It results in a reasonable estimate of how many additional sales dollars the promotion will have to generate in order to cover its costs and show a profit.

Example A
_____

PRE-PROMOTIONAL PAYOUT ANALYSIS

Promotion Objective.
   Increase sales by 10 percent during a four-week period.
Promotion Description.
   Every customer purchasing a submarine sandwich priced at $2.50 or more will receive a side-order item valued at 50¢ free (cole slaw, potato salad, baked beans, etc.).

Assumptions.

Promotion will bring in 480 additional customers over 4 weeks to purchase sandwiches.

Store Sales.

Currently averaging $6,000 a week.

Promotional Costs (projected):

- Newspaper ads—$100
- Food cost of 480 additional side-order items at 20¢ each—$96
- Point of purchase materials—$100
- Total promotional cost—$296

Payout

- Necessary incremental sales to payout
- $296 divided by 40 percent (gross profit) = payout of $740
- $740 divided by $24,000 (four weeks' sales) Necessary Sales Increase to Payout = 3.08 percent

or

- Increase sales by more than 3.08 percent to payout (or show a profit)

To show a profit, based on a 40 percent pre-tax profit factor, sales must increase by 3.08 percent.

The information obtained through similar calculations based on your planned promotion will put you in a position to judge more clearly whether the promotion's chances of profitability are sound.

Promotional Evaluation

This is a measure of a promotion's results in terms of pressure points on overall sales. In the following example let's see how our sandwich promotion did as far as net profits are concerned.

Example B

SUBMARINE SANDWICH RESTAURANT

Promotion Description.
Every customer purchasing a sandwich priced at $2.50 or more will receive a side-order item valued at 50¢ (retail) free for a four-week period.

	Week #1	Week #2	Week #3	Week #4
Total sandwich sales with side-orders	$360	$252	$180	$120
Free side-order items distributed	144	101	72	48
Total promotional food cost (20¢ per item)	$ 28.80	$ 20.20	$ 14.40	$ 9.60

Four-week Total
Sandwich sales (with side-order items) **$912**. Free side-order items distributed **365**. Total food cost **$73.00**

Promotional Costs.
Newspaper ads $100; point of purchase $100; cost of free food $73.00; *Total:* $273.00

Sales-Income
Total promotional sales over four weeks is equal to

$912 x 40 percent pre-tax profit equals $364.80

$364.80 (Promotional Sales)
- 273.00 (Promotional Costs)
$91.80 Net Profit

As you can see, net profit to the restaurant over the promotional period of four weeks was $91.80. But we have to go further still and analyze total net sales. This is accomplished by first determining the average of store sales over four "normal" non-promotional weeks prior to your promotional period. This will serve as a benchmark against which to measure the promotional results. A similar calculation for a four-week, post-promotional period gives us still another perspective on the impact of the promotion.

Example C

EVALUATION OF TOTAL NET SALES

Base Period	Net Sales	% + or - vs. base	% + or - vs. promo period
Average 4 weeks' sales prior to promotional period	$6,000		
Promotional Period			
Week #1	$7,100	+ 18%	
Week #2	6,800	+ 13%	
Week #3	6,500	+ 8%	
Week #4	6,250	+ 4%	
Promotional Average	$6,662.50	+ 11%	
Post-Promotional Average	$6,300	5%	(-5.4%)

Conclusions
1. Total sales increased 11 percent during promotional period and
2. Post promotional average indicated a (5.4%) decrease against the promotional period, but sales still maintained a 5% increase over the base period.

EVALUATION OF TRANSACTION COUNT

Base Period	Customers per Week	% + or - vs. base	% + or - vs. promo period
Four-week average previous to the promotion	2,500		
Promotion Period			
Week #1	3,155	26.2%	
Week #2	3,022	20.8%	
Week #3	2,888	15.5%	
Week #4	2,777	11.1%	
Promotional Average	2,960	18.4%	
Post-Promotional Average (four weeks post)	2,750	10%	(-7.1%)

The final step in the evaluation process is to compare how the actual promotion compares with the original payout projection.

Example D

POST-PROMOTIONAL PAYOUT ANALYSIS

Based on $6,000 a week or $24,000 for four weeks

Projected	Actual
Promotional Costs: $296	Promotional Costs: $273.00
Necessary Sales to Payout = $740	
Increase Sales by 3.08% to Payout	Actual sales increased by 11%!

You can see that to accumulate the necessary data for these calculations you have to monitor the promotion carefully while it is in progress.

You have now been introduced to the Seven Keys to neighborhood-restaurant marketing. In subsequent chapters you will learn about what you need to turn these keys successfully and to unlock the door to higher profits. Before we go on, though, I want to touch briefly on still another important subject: *communication.*

As you prepare to implement a neighborhood-restaurant marketing plan, you should also prepare to communicate that plan to those who work for you. You should tell all your employees that you are taking a new direction in marketing. You should then tell them exactly what part you expect them to take in helping you make that direction pay off for all of you. Neighborhood-restaurant marketing will not work unless you familiarize all your employees with its guiding principles. It is not enough for you alone to know what neighborhood-restaurant marketing is all about. You must share that knowledge *selectively* but *thoroughly.*

advertising: paying the least— getting the most

NOW that you have chosen the tactical elements of your marketing plan, you must let your target audience know what you are going to offer them. You're about to step into the world of advertising. The most important thing to remember as you take this step is that it will not put you on Madison Avenue but on the "Main Street" in your community. You haven't the resources for Madison Avenue glamour, but you can afford Main Street practicality. In fact, you can't afford to ignore it.

In your store and through locally available media you can reach the people in your neighborhood-restaurant marketing trading area. It's likely that you've already done some advertising. But even if you have, this chapter will give you a new perspective on what you've been doing and point the way to new and economical techniques. If you've shied away from advertising because you've lacked confidence in your ability to do this job well, this chapter will help you remedy that situation. The following pages will list available media and methods for getting the most from them.

NEWSPAPERS

Newspapers are excellent vehicles for delivering messages. But be prepared to shop around for your best buy in terms of cost and coverage. Many daily newspapers cover broad metropolitan markets, so advertising costs are high. Thus, paying to advertise beyond your trading area wastes your money. However, these larger papers often run zone editions and weekly or bi-weekly suburban supplements. If this is the case in your area, be sure to investigate the possibilities of advertising in these supplements

There are an increasing number of regional papers being published by newspaper chains. If one of these papers covers your community, you may want to check out its space rates as they may prove quite reasonable. Also, there is a chance that if your promotions are as strong as they should be, you may attract customers from beyond your usual trading area. However, local papers, with circulations of between 8,000 and 10,000, are probably your best bet.

In addition, there are other publications that may have little or no editorial content and may be properly classified as "penny-savers." These usually are available free-of-charge at local retailers or supermarkets with high traffic volumes. They may even be delivered door-to-door.

These community papers and penny-savers are prime vehicles for neighborhood-restaurant marketing. If both exist in your area you may want to use them simultaneously for reasonably priced coverage and for reinforcing your message by repetition.

The following material will show you how to maximize effective usage of these media.

Planning Your Newspaper Campaign

Once you've decided to place an ad, there are some additional factors to be considered:

- Cost
- Discounts
- Ad size
- Placement/position
- Frequency of insertion
- Creation of the ad
- Black and white versus color

Cost. Newspaper space may be purchased in any one of the following ways:

- *Per Line.* The term is *agate line* and it represents the depth of space on a page. To determine total cost, simply multiply the line rate by the total number of lines (for example, $.12 x 600 lines = $72).
- *Column Inch.* Simply multiply the number of columns by the depth of the ad in inches, then multiply the per-column-inch rate by the total number of column inches (for example, 4 col. x 10 in. = 40 col./in. @ $4.25 an inch = $170).
- *Size of Page.* Many smaller newspapers sell space for a flat fee based on ad size (for example, ¼ page = $150).

Discounts. Certain discounts may be obtained to achieve greater cost efficiency. By planning ahead in terms of the total amount of space or number of insertions over a given period of time (usually one year), you can obtain more favorable contract rates from local newspapers.

Ad Size. Determining the ad size will depend on the budget and the creative requirements necessary to communicate the information to the consumer. For the purposes of local marketing, the most popular ad size is 600 lines—approximately half a page. In a tabloid size paper a quarter page is standard.

Placement/Position. In newspapers—as opposed to pennysavers—the placement of the ad in a particular section will determine the type of person most likely to read the ad. Therefore, if the ad is targeted toward men, you should request that it be placed either in the general news or sports sections. An ad targeted toward women should be placed in the lifestyle, fashion, or food sections. Although newspapers have the freedom of placing the ad in any section they choose, most papers will try to honor your request. Some will ask extra payment for specific placement.

Frequency. The frequency with which an ad is inserted is predicated on the budget, as well as the objective you wish to achieve. For example, an ad carrying a special coupon offer designed to achieve an immediate sales "bounce" should only be inserted once during the redemption period of the coupon. If the ad is designed to support a four-week promotional effort and the objective is to have customers visit frequently, the newspaper ad should be inserted during the first and third weeks of the promotion.

Creating the Ad. Any newspaper ad consists of a combination of two basic elements: copy and art. The copy includes all the words in the ad and the art is the illustration. Newspapers usually have an art department capable of helping you create your ad, often at no additional cost once you've placed a space order.

The best procedure for you to follow is to write out what thoughts you want your ad to convey. Keep the copy simple and direct, making sure you include all the pertinent information. After this is done, you may want to try to develop a tasteful but attention-getting headline. You may also want to rough out a layout if you can visualize how you would like the ad to look.

Then, meet with your newspaper space rep who will then review the concept you have drawn up and make suggestions for improvement. Once both of you have agreed on a basic approach, the rep can take the ad back to the art department for refinement and completion.

Be sure to approve the ad in final form before it is published.

If you already have some form of existing artwork (your restaurant's logo or restaurant symbol, for example), give it to the rep and ask him or her to include it in the layout.

Incorporation of a coupon is usually a good idea for newspaper ads. Not only will a coupon bring customers to the store but it will also provide a way to evaluate the ad and the promotion it supports.

Black and White versus Color. Although studies indicate color ads enhance readership, the use of color will add significantly to the cost of the ad (if color is even available in your particular local papers). Therefore, for neighborhood-restaurant marketing, I recommend black and white ads only.

RADIO

Advertising on radio is an excellent way to penetrate the local market and yet it is often overlooked—perhaps because it is regarded as being far more costly and more difficult to arrange than it actually is.

Not only is radio advertising cost-efficient in terms of coverage, it possesses the advantages of timeliness and flexibility. It's possible to think today of a message you want to communicate and have it on the air by tomorrow!

Beyond this, radio offers a tremendous opportunity for audience segmentation. If you define your ideal promotion target as, say, women between the ages of 18 and 34, you can probably find a station whose format caters to that particular group. There are rock stations for teenagers and sports stations for men, FM stations featuring classical music, and ethnic stations. Many stations cover specific community areas and small towns. You can determine audience peak times as well. Switch on your radio and tune from station to station on the AM and FM bands to confirm this information. This will also give you a good idea of the extent of the competition between stations that helps to keep prices down.

Radio usage is high because people listen while working and relaxing, as well as when driving—and they may be driving to shop in your trading area. You can use radio to offer what amounts to over-the-air coupons: "If you buy something from XYZ Company during this special promotion, tell them you heard this announcement and you'll receive a free T-shirt (comb, glass of wine, etc.)."

Don't attempt to use radio for extensive details. It won't work. Because radio commercials are only thirty or sixty seconds long, they are best used for top-line awareness of your restaurant and products. They are reasonably priced and are proven complements to more detailed newspaper advertising.

Planning Your Radio Campaign

When planning radio usage, review the following factors:

- Station choice
- Commercial length
- Quantity (repetition) scheduling
- Creating the commercial
- Cost

Choosing the right station. First, decide on the target audience you want to reach (i.e., teenagers, women 18 to 49, etc.). Then call the radio stations in your area and talk with the sales representatives. Each station has a demographic breakout of their audience and will be glad to show it to you. When selecting a station, also consider the station's rating—its position in the market relative to the other stations. Ratings are measured in fifteen-minute increments. All you really need to know about ratings is that the higher the rating, the more people reached and the more a spot costs.

After talking to all the station reps and learning their target audiences and ratings, you may decide to advertise on more than one station in order to increase your impact on your chosen target market.

Selecting the length of the radio commercial. Practically speaking, radio spots come in two lengths, thirty seconds and sixty seconds. Naturally, the type of spot you select will depend on your budget and on the type of message you wish to advertise. Most of the time sixty-second spots will be a better buy than thirty-second spots because you'll have more time to deliver your message and because a thirty second rate usually ranges from 70 to 80 percent of a sixty second rate. It usually works out that you can buy twice as much time per spot and pay only about one-and-a-quarter to one-and-a-half times as much.

Quantity scheduling. Many advertisers prefer to place their spots during the two highest radio circulation periods: the morning drive time, 6 AM to 10 AM, or the afternoon drive time, 3 PM to 7 PM. These periods capitalize on the largest segment of the home-to-work and work-to-home audiences. But, of course, these periods are also the most expensive. To achieve greater cost efficiency, it's best to spread your spots between the major drive periods and the other listening periods of the day (10 AM to 3 PM, 7 PM to 12 midnite, and 12 midnite to 6 AM.

To attain meaningful promotional weight you should consider a schedule of twenty-five spots per station per week if you purchase multiple stations. Fifteen spots will do the job if you choose only one station.

Creating the commercial. There are a number of types of radio spots:

1. *Live Spot.* This spot is the simplest to produce because the announcer merely reads the radio copy live on-air. Sometimes the copy is read over a musical background to add to audience appeal. This is the most inexpensive spot to create because most of the time there is no production cost at all. This spot is highly recommended for local marketing purposes.
2. *"Canned" or Produced Spot.* This is recorded on tape and simply forwarded to the station for playing. These can be very elaborate and include jingles, extensive orchestration, or special sound effects.

They are usually produced by a commercial production house and can be quite costly for one spot.

3. *The Donut.* This involves a produced opening and a produced closing with a hole in the middle so the announcer can read live copy. This is probably the most flexible type of spot since you only have it produced once but can change the live copy to coincide with whatever promotion you want to run. This type of spot is normally not too expensive to produce, because the cost may be spread out over many commercials.

Copy preparation is usually a minimal problem because most radio stations will write your copy free. Just describe the details of your program to the sales rep and he or she will have the copy written at the station. Again, make sure you approve the copy and check your spots occasionally to see that they are run on time as approved.

Cost. As we've discussed, radio cost is dependent on station rating, spot length, and spot scheduling. But there are other factors you should be aware of. Radio stations compete aggressively for the advertising dollar and most of them will negotiate off their standard rate card if business is slow.

Don't immediately settle for the price on the rate card. Tell the rep your budget can't accommodate that figure. Many times, in the hope of future business—and depending on the station's inventory of unsold time—you might be offered a better deal.

Also ask about the station's discount policy. If you sign a contract agreeing to run a specified number of spots over a period of time, your cost per spot should drop considerably.

For additional economy, be aware that if you place the advertising directly with the station, instead of going through an ad agency, you pay the non-commissionable (net) rate which is usually at least 15 percent less.

To re-emphasize: Properly used radio can be a very effective means of advertising your restaurant and product. But don't pay for circulation that won't benefit you. Make sure you're buying a radio station that has at least 80 percent of its coverage in the trading area you want to reach.

BILLBOARDS AND MOBILE BILLBOARDS

There are several forms of outdoor advertising you should think about:

Billboards. Paper billboard space is usually sold by the month and may be illuminated or not. Billboards' primary usage should be as directional signs to attract traffic from major arteries to your store. Usually the outdoor company can handle production of the poster at an additional cost. Painted boards are usually sold on a one or three year contract. Rotator boards are also available for purchase. In a rotator showing, board locations will change every sixty days.

Mobile Billboards. Mounted on vans or towed on trailers, mobile billboards are rented by the day, week, or month and can be equipped with sound.

DOORKNOB HANGERS

House-to-house distribution of doorknob hangers can be useful to advertise special events such as anniversaries or a celebrity appearance. They lend themselves especially well to couponing.

Doorknob hangers are hard to miss and they reach potential customers at home with an effect much like direct mail, while costing much less than direct mail. For specific timing, they circumvent the competitive clutter of newspapers or mailing pieces. Moreover, distribution is focused and controlled—you pick the residential areas that you want to reach.

There are professional doorknob hanger services; they usually charge a flat rate per thousand hangers distributed. You may want to use local youth organizations for the distribution, contributing funds to Scout troops or 4-H Club members for this service. If the group wears their uniforms or other identification when distributing your hangers, you gain credibility. You may also receive a bonus by being recognized as a supporter of youth activities.

If you have young staff members, you may want to set up incentive competition between them, having each member deliver color-coded coupon hangers and devising a way to rate their success. Naturally, winners should be rewarded!

YELLOW PAGES

The classified telephone directory is valuable for businesses of all types and sizes and for several extremely cogent reasons:

1. Yellow pages are used *after* the consumer has made a decision to buy.
2. They offer broad market coverage.
3. They are as available as the telephone. Virtually every household and business has one. Over 150,000,000 copies of Yellow Page directories are distributed annually.
4. They offer a range of advertising formats from single-line items to full-page display ads.
5. They're accessible to you. Just contact your local Yellow Pages rep for detailed information and assistance.

Although each advertising method has been discussed separately, coupling different methods (e.g. newspaper and radio ads) creates reinforcement and continuity, which you should always try to build into your advertising. Coupling methods builds a stronger, more visible image and may be achieved through using any combination of the methods discussed.

Remember, though, that the key to this reinforcement is the use of common elements. Your restaurant's name is naturally one of these. A simple, catchy slogan—or in print ads, an eye-catching logo or symbol—will do the job. This tying together of messages through common elements and the use of multiple media will result in the development of an organized campaign—and an instrument of maximum impact.

A highly sophisticated, successful, and consequently visible example of an ad campaign is AT&T's pervasive "Reach out and Touch Someone" concept. Carried out through all levels of advertising—TV, radio, newspapers, magazines, Bell System bill stuffers, signs in Bell Company office buildings and inside PhoneCenter Stores—the Reach Out theme has undergone endless attractive variations.

You've probably noted by now that I have only mentioned TV once in this chapter. The omission was entirely intentional. TV is not for neighborhood-restaurant marketing, with just a single exception: If you are part of a national franchise chain, you will naturally include in your advertising elements that will "piggy-back" on TV advertising or other national or regional media usage.

MEASURING RESULTS VS. COSTS

You must always try to measure the effectiveness of your advertising to see how well you are spending your ad dollars. Some forms of advertising may be harder to evaluate than others, but there are some standard measures.

1. Before buying any media, always compare the
   cost per thousand. This is the oldest accepted
   standard of media efficiency. The cost of the

media is divided by the estimated audience to produce a cost per thousand (CPM) figure. For example, the $200 cost of a newspaper ad divided by a 10,000 circulation gives a $.50 CPM.

2. *What sales are traceable to media?* Simply track all sales and attribute them as closely as possible to a particular advertising medium. As indicated previously, this is easily done with print coupons where you only have to tabulate the response by totalling coupons redeemed and having your employees record the total sale that each coupon brought in.

In the case of more than one print ad running at the same time, simply code the coupon in each paper with a letter or number to trace back to the appropriate newspaper.

With radio it's a little more difficult but it can still be accomplished. If you make a special offer on your radio spot as suggested earlier, have your employees record each mention of the station by customers. After completing your advertising, total the amount of sales brought in by the promotion as a whole. Then break out each advertising vehicle by sales and index it to the total.

3. *What were sales per each dollar of investment?* This is another means of measuring the return on advertising investment. Simply total all sales traceable to a single type of media by sales category. Then divide each category by the cost of that particular medium.

I think it was Henry Ford that said, "50 percent of my advertising is wasted, but I don't know which 50 percent it is." Not very comforting, but that statement indicates the difficulty of evaluating your advertising. But you must advertise! And you must evaluate!

In this chapter I have concentrated on what you can accomplish through your own advertising efforts. But I want to conclude with some cautionary advice: Depending on the size of your business and available resources, you might find that the cost of engaging a reputable advertising agency is well justified.

sales building PROMOTION STRATEGIES

chApter seven

TO many people, advertising and sales promotions are just about the same thing. True, they will share the same bottom line purpose: to improve your restaurant's business. But, even though advertising and sales promotions do, and should, complement each other, they are separate disciplines.

Perhaps one way of distinguishing them is to say advertising creates overall awareness, while promotion is aimed directly at stimulating sales of specific products at a specific time. Advertising presents the proposition, sales promotions close the deal. An easy way to view the distinction is to see how both disciplines are executed. In the previous chapter, I described advertising in detail. This chapter details the most important classes of sales promotion tools and activities.

POINT OF PURCHASE/POINT OF SALE

Creating a demand for a product or service through successful advertising is usually not enough to make the sale. Restaurant-level reinforcement of the advertising message is necessary and is the prime function of point-of-purchase (P.O.P.) which are often referred to in industry as Point of Sale (P.O.S.) materials. A second major function of these materials is to stimulate impulse buying. Research indicates that as much as 51 percent of all impulse buying is created by P.O.P. display.

Following are the standard types of P.O.P. materials:

- Window Displays
- Wall Posters & Hangers
- Counter Cards
- Counter Displays
- Window and Door Stickers
- Floor Displays
- Bagstuffers
- Banners

Naturally, the type of P.O.P. materials required will depend on the type of promotion and, of course, budget. Creating P.O.P. materials can be expensive. One way to defray cost is to contact the manufacturer's representative of the products you are promoting. Many major suppliers or vendors have standard P.O.P. materials available to restaurant operators at little or no expense. (For example, Coke has complete P.O.P. kits, including posters, counter cards, and mobiles, etc., showing Coke with various product combinations—hamburgers, subs, chicken.) Depending on your volume with that particular supplier, you may be able to obtain a promotional allowance to help cover the cost of special P.O.P. production. Many of the soft drink companies have rebate programs or co-op ad programs based on the amount of gallons used.

Here are some tips on proper in-restaurant placement of P.O.P.:

1. Study the layout of your restaurant and determine optimum display points based on customer traffic and access. Behind the serving counter is an excellent place for P.O.P.

2. Position P.O.P. materials where they can be readily seen by the customers. However, avoid interference with actual serving areas.
3. Place P.O.P. displays in well-lit areas.
4. Try and unify all P.O.P. into one cohesive visual theme.
5. Regard P.O.P. as a "silent sales rep" who can significantly affect sales of specific products and cause positive changes in the overall product mix over a period of time.
6. Rotate P.O.P. at least every month in order to maintain customer interest. Moreover, it should dovetail with advertising.

DIRECT MAIL

A properly executed direct mail program can be one of your most successful neighborhood-restaurant-marketing tools in terms of creating mass impact on a large number of people in the shortest amount of time.

Direct Mail

- Pinpoints marketing to specific target audiences, including special geographic and demographic targeting.
- Eliminates wasteful circulation of mass media.
- Lends itself to controlled timing.

Direct Mail Planning

If you answer any of these questions with a resounding yes, you should seriously consider direct mail:

- Is there a residential area within your trading area where you want to increase penetration?
- Is yours a new restaurant in the trading area?

- Do you have a particular sales period that needs strengthening?
- Do you have one particular product that needs promotional emphasis?
- Have you introduced a new product for which you are trying to build a market?

The most important aspect of direct mail is its vigorous generation of high amounts of restaurant traffic. The critical elements of direct mail are:

- Choice of Offer
- Choice of Mail House
- Budget
- Evaluation
- Creative

Selecting an Offer

Your offer must be strong enough to entice a good response or all your direct mail dollars will be wasted. When selecting offers you should always select your most popular items, the ones you can always depend on. The entire mailing piece need not be devoted to these items but they certainly should be prominent.

Consider the profitability of the products involved. This will help you decide to offer the product free, free with a purchase, or as a special discounted offer. The rule of thumb is to select offers sufficiently popular to *draw customers* but in a way that will at least cover your product cost even though you may show a loss on paper. The idea is to generate enough *additional sales* through *additional purchases* to offset any loss from the special offer and to cover the entire cost of the program.

For example, if you send out a mailer offering a $5.00 dinner that normally sells for $10.00 retail, you should pick up an additional $5.00 in sales from every customer redeeming the coupon to make up your profit loss of $5.00 per dinner. However, because the dinner actually cost you only $5.00, you do not *lose any money* on the dinner.

Always determine the projected sales and costs of a mailer to ascertain the total amount of sales needed to make the mailer a profitable investment. For example, let's assume the total cost of a mailer is $5,000 and your gross profit is 50 percent. That means in order to justify the cost, the mailer would have to generate $10,000 in gross sales. You must determine if this is a realistic rate of return for your situation.

Choosing a Mail House. Careful selection of a mail house is essential to the success of your program. Shop for the right mail house, keeping the following in mind:

Costs. Mail house costs include a fee for list rental and another fee for the labeling, tying, bagging, and delivering your piece to the Post Office. These fees are charged on a cost-per-thousand basis, normally about $15.00 C.P.M. This does not include postage, which is always billed as a separate charge based on how the mailer is to be sent. Most mailers are sent third class bulk. Make sure you get thorough, comparable cost breakdowns from each mail house.

List Currency. Find out how often the mail houses you're considering update their residence lists.

Timing. Find out how much lead time the mail houses need to process and mail your pieces.

Regulations. The mail house selected should be up-to-date on the latest postal regulations so that your mail piece will conform to those regulations.

Knowledgability. Check how well the mail houses know the general area to be covered by the mailing. This is especially helpful in the case of multiple units where you don't want to infringe on another restaurant's trading area.

Preparing the Piece

You should always try to put out the best quality mailing piece you can afford. The mailer represents you and your restaurant!

1. Prepare your own rough copy and layout. State your offer boldly and unmistakeably in the headline. Include an expiration date. Be certain each offer indicates that the offer is good only at your address.
2. Get a count from the mail house on the quantity to be mailed.
3. Order the appropriate quantity of pieces from a local printer (use the printer's art or layout facilities to develop a finished production layout) and decide on the printing process and type of stock (if possible, use four-color printing since it usually gets a better response).
4. Check finished layout and copy *before* production. Check printed pieces for accuracy and quality before the printer delivers the pieces to the mail house.
5. On the average, a direct mail program takes approximately four to six weeks to implement.

Establishing a Budget

Always determine the total number of pieces to be mailed on a cost-per-thousand basis to include mailing costs, printing costs, and the cost of the merchandise used in promotion.

Evaluating Results

Always record the total number of coupons redeemed. To determine the total income from the promotion, record add-on sales from each coupon. (These are sales over and above any mandatory coupon purchase.) Determine the gross profit margin of total sales, and then subtract all promotional costs to find your net profit.

RETAIL TIE-INS

Tying in with other retailers is a good way to extend your advertising impact and to get more mileage from your advertising budget. A properly planned joint promotion takes advantage of the different aspects of each partner's business.

Consider these factors when planning a joint promotion:

1. Determine what benefit you want from your promotional partner (i.e., traffic, advertising, merchandise, etc.).
2. Make sure your promotional partner has a quality reputation.
3. Be sure that you and the tie-in partner have the same target audience.
4. The most successful joint promotions are those that both parties benefit from equally. Be fair when you negotiate the terms of the partnership.

PERSONAL APPEARANCES

Selecting a Celebrity

Having a celebrity appear at your restaurant can be a great source of excitement, sales, and traffic. But it's important to choose a celebrity who will fit your needs and image. Popular local television and radio personalities are excellent candidates for personal appearances.

Cost is certainly a factor since celebrities can charge anywhere from a few hundred to several thousand dollars. For that money you should expect the best possible show. State exactly what you expect the celebrity to do and how long the appearance will last. Do not be intimidated by the celebrity's reputation or by his or her agent. They are in the market to sell their services and you're the customer.

Planning the Personal Appearance

Once you've made an agreement, carefully plan the appearance. Keep in mind how you can best use the celebrity's personality.

1. Decide where the appearance will take place.
   Will it be inside your restaurant or outside, in your parking lot or on the street? Should you combine locations? Remember you want to place the celebrity where there is maximum visibility and where interference with selling and customer service is at a minimum.
2. Set up an agenda/timetable for each activity during the appearance. Decide if the celebrity will perform the same activity during the entire appearance or if there will be changes.
3. Time all advertising to give adequate advance notice of the appearance. Repetition over a two-week period should work well.
4. Order supporting in-store point of purchase materials.
5. Inform your employees of the details of the promotion and their involvement in it.
6. Contact local police to see if any permits are necessary and to advise them of the possibility of traffic control problems. If it seems necessary, request traffic control support.
7. Obtain any necessary sound equipment, portable stage, seats, etc.
8. Reconfirm all appearance details with the celebrity or the agent.

Get the maximum benefit from your promotion!! For best results schedule the appearance on a weekend. Try to work the celebrity appearance into a promotional activity (i.e., run a Sweepstakes and have the celebrity draw the winners).

PRODUCT PROMOTIONS

Discounting

Discounting can be a very effective promotional device, but it must not be carried to extremes.

Over-frequent product discounting can diminish the value of the product when you return to charging your usual prices. Consumers have a tendency to alter their purchase patterns to wait and see if the discount price will be available again.

When possible, offer the discount in the form of "free with the purchase of," or "buy one/get one free." Omitting any mention of price prevents erosion of consumers' perceptions of the value of your products.

Price and Item

Promotion of a specific product at a specific price is called *price* and *item advertising*. This form of advertising can be very useful in new product introductions or in competitive promotions that call special attention to a familiar product at a special competitive price (i.e., offering a roast beef sandwich for $1.50 when it would normally sell for $2.25). Always support price and item advertising with prominent in-store P.O.P. displays featuring the advertised product.

SWEEPSTAKES

Sweepstakes can be a very effective way of creating excitement and building traffic and sales.

Selection of Prizes

Obviously, you must match the prize to the audience. Don't offer a vacation if your target audience is children. Each prize structure should contain a Grand Prize supported by one or two major prizes and a greater quantity of smaller prizes.

As always, try to contain costs, but don't sacrifice your image of quality. One way to obtain prizes at reduced costs or no cost is to tie-in with another retailer who will provide them in return for promotional consideration.

Usually, the more prizes the better. If a customer thinks there is a good chance of winning because there are a lot of prizes, he will be more likely to enter.

Creation of Materials

To run a sweepstakes all you really need is an entry blank and P.O.P. in the form of counter cards and posters.

The entry blank should contain the name of the sweepstakes, the prize offered, where to enter, and the rules (which must contain a deadline for entries and a drawing date). Because the entry blanks should be distributed over the counter to your customers, you will need approximate traffic counts to determine the quantity of entry blanks to be printed. Display the prizes inside the restaurant when possible.

Advertising

Sweepstakes should always be advertised to the *general public* as opposed to being offered only to your own customers.

A sweepstakes should run for at least four weeks, with newspaper advertising appearing at the beginning of each week of the contest. If radio is used, a minimum of twenty-five spots per week should be scheduled.

In all your advertising be sure to sell the prizes and urge your customers—and prospective customers—to enter at *your* restaurant if a number of restaurants are involved in the sweepstakes.

The Drawing

1. Stick to the publicized time and date of the drawing *no matter what happens.* Your credibility is at stake, and it's the law.
2. Try to get a local dignitary to select the winners. However, a customer chosen at random to draw the winners will add to your credibility. Don't forget the previous suggestion of having a local celebrity such as a pro athlete or a popular TV or radio personality to do the honors.
3. Have a photographer on hand when the winners pick up their prizes. Send the photos to the local press. They make good human interest features and extend the visibility of your restaurant.

Legal Aspects of a Sweepstakes

Before planning any sweepstakes, check your state's lottery laws for the rules governing sweepstakes. In most states, requiring a purchase is illegal. Check with your attorney for legal restrictions before implementing any sweepstakes promotion.

ADVERTISING SPECIALTIES

Free Give-Aways

Low cost specialty items have a number of uses. They are often used to reward your customers for their patronage. Although a free key chain may not seem like much in itself, the customer goodwill and interest created by these novelties can be well worth the investment.

Whatever specialties you use should carry an imprint of your business name and address as a reminder of where they came from. Periodically, incorporate use of advertising specialties into your existing advertising.

Specialty items can spur sales during specific day parts or days of the week. Advertising specialties have great appeal among children and may attract adults through appealing to their children.

Here are some suggested specialty items:

- Pens
- Pencils
- Memo/Address Books
- Calendars
- Beach Toys
- Windshield Scrapers
- Key Chains
- Desk Accessories
- Book Covers
- Crayons/Coloring Books
- Potholders

Self-Liquidators

A self-liquidator is a more expensive advertising specialty item that is not given but sold to the consumer at the price it cost the retailer. The object is merely to cover the cost of the item with a required purchase and to reap a profit with resultant add-on sales.

For example, a fast-food chain offers a drinking glass for thirty-nine cents, the price it paid for the item. However, the average purchase during the promotion ran to about $2.50. This means that the average consumer spent $2.11 in addition to the cost of the glass.

Several well-timed and well-advertised self-liquidation promotions can attract additional customers by providing an additional reason for visiting your particular store. Going a step further, you can create a frequency promotion by encouraging customers to collect an entire set of self-liquidators by offering a different one each week for a four-or-five-week period.

IN-STORE ACTIVITIES

In-store promotions generate new customers as well as additional visits from your current customer base. They are inexpensive and don't require a great deal of effort to execute. None of these promotions will generate tremendous sales on its own, but the cumulative effect of constant promotion will pay off. These programs do not require much advertising and can be executed with basic in-store P.O.P. materials such as bag stuffers and counter cards.

There are many varieties of in-store activities. Here are a few examples.

Tennis or Racquetball Clinic. Ask a pro from a local tennis or racquetball club to give a talk on the fundamentals of his or her particular sport. The pro can answer questions on technique and equipment and may want to distribute discount coupons for lessons at the club. This same type of clinic can be set up for down-hill or cross-country skiing by exchanging the services of a local ski shop owner for in-store publicity.

Foil-a-Thief Day. Engraving social security numbers or initials on C.B.'s, portable radios, and tape recorders can help recover stolen items. With an electric engraving pen, have one of your employees put this information on valuables for customers. This can increase customer traffic, plus act as an important community service.

Caricature Night. Caricaturists draw attention wherever they work. Hire a talented high school or college student to draw caricatures of your customers. This is a good event to repeat, because those who attend your first Caricature Night will get the word (and their pictures) around very quickly.

You get the general idea. Put your imagination to work on in-store activities that might pertain particularly to your business or that have seasonal or specialized interest: A Flower Seed Day, Career Afternoon, Celebrity Look-Alike Day, or a Senior Citizen Day.

FREQUENCY DEVICE

A promotional frequency device is designed to bring a customer back to your restaurant a specific number of times over a given period.

As has been said before, if each of your customers visited your restaurant just one extra time each month, you would increase your volume by 50 percent. Two excellent frequency devices are punch cards and bounce-back coupons.

There are several different types of punch cards. Some are based on a specific purchase amount, others on specific product purchases.

Basically, customers are given a card with a certain number of boxes, usually five or ten, depending on the length of the promotion. Each time the customer presents his card and makes the required purchase, his or her card is punched or validated. When all the boxes are completed, the card is then redeemed for a free product. Punch-card pay out is excellent, since many people will complete 50 percent to 75 percent of the required purchases but will not keep the card long enough to redeem it for the free offer. Even if the card is redeemed, profit on the required purchase will more than offset the cost of the free offer. (For example, hand out a five-box punch card. Each time a customer makes a $3.00 purchase, the card is validated. After the card is completed, it is redeemed on the sixth visit for a free dinner for two.)

Cards should be distributed and validated for a four-week period and then be redeemable during the following two-week period.

Another standard frequency device is the bounce-back coupon. Distributed over-the-counter, these invite your customers to return during a designated day or part of a day to take advantage of a special offer. This is a good way to use strong sales periods to help build weaker ones. For example, if you would like to build weekday business, distribute a bounce-back coupon on the weekends good only on the weekdays.

Sales promotion activities should be an integral part of your total neighborhood-restaurant marketing plan. The benefits derived will only depend on your own creativity and the proper targeting of these activities to meet the overall stated objectives.

PROjECTiNG AND PROTECTiNG yOUR RESTAURANT'S iMAGE

CHAPTER EIGHT

THERE are so many definitions, purposes, and branches of public relations that even professionals in the field have difficulty in sorting them out. For retailers engaged in neighborhood-restaurant marketing, however, a specific branch of public relations can be isolated as being of prime importance. That branch is community relations.

The purpose of community relations is to create a positive image of you and your business in your trading area. These activities supplement your sales promotion activities by promoting you as a person to be highly trusted. You will be thought of as a community member concerned with returning to the community a fair portion of the benefits you derive from it.

THE POWER OF TRUST

To illustrate the potential power of trust here is a story about how a major food chain's reputation superseded some bad publicity it received a while back. The company was running a major promotion involving the sale of decorated drinking glasses. Several million glasses were produced and a follow-up promotion involving dinner plates was planned, with the production order again totaling several million. The glass promotion was into its final weeks when a story broke in Massachusetts that the state had stopped the promotion there. It was alleged that the dye used in decorating the glasses could be unsafe if swallowed.

The ramifications were obvious and threatening. Millions of dollars could be lost through refunds on the glasses and the unused plates. Most important, what about the goodwill this chain had carefully nurtured over the years?

To shorten a complicated story, the chain proved to the state that the dye had been thoroughly tested before use and was indeed safe. The Massachusetts ban was rescinded. But, as often happens, there was minimal publicity about the exoneration of the firm. So the question remained: How would customers react? Should the plate promotion go on?

It was revealed that *through activities on the community level* the restaurant chain had built up more trust than the government agencies dedicated to watching out for the public interest. Despite all its threats of serious consumer problems, the situation left the chain virtually unscathed.

Of course, this case was extreme. You'll probably never be faced with a disaster of that magnitude. But consider this: would your reputation sustain you in the face of adverse public comments by local health officials? What if an impatient employee was rude to an elderly person active in a Senior Citizens Club? If you have proved your good will through recognized community action, you should find that your reputation will have earned you fair opportunity for rebuttal or apology— whichever was appropriate.

BUILDING A POSITIVE IMAGE

However, in addition to providing "insurance," positive community relations creates trading area recognition. You have a vehicle for publicizing your name to customers and non-customers alike. You will build trust which, of course, builds sales.

Retailers often neglect community relations because they don't appreciate its value, which is mostly intangible and can't be precisely measured. The value is real. Don't let your competition beat you to the punch in the battle for community recognition.

You can't create a positive community image overnight—unless you happen to rescue some children from drowning. Even at that, you'd have to work hard to keep that heroic image alive. Moreover, community relations should not be attempted as a series of sporadic efforts. It should be carefully planned.

Your approach to community relations should be pragmatic and practical. Remember, only part of your goal is to become *involved* in community activities. The other part is to be *recognized* for that involvement.

Planning Community Involvement

Opportunities for community relations abound. No doubt you are already besieged with requests to support and participate in activities and projects by such organizations and institutions as churches, hospitals, the Scouts and Little Leagues. In most cases you are asked to donate money or to help raise it. You must carefully choose which activities to undertake and what form of involvement will benefit both the community and your business. When you plan community involvement consider these seven points.

What do you want to accomplish for your business? First, remember that there's nothing wrong with being charitable and benefiting from it; but be tasteful about it. Decide whether you want community-wide recognition or association with a particular group or event. Is there a specific image problem relating to your business that you can counter by a given type of involvement?

How well is the group organized? Be wary of joining a project that you may have to take total control over to ensure its success. Check to see if the group is sufficiently staffed and organized to carry out a project. Contribute your time and energy as necessary, but make sure they're in proportion to your goals. Don't take too much time from your other responsibilities.

Determine if the goal of the project is realistic! Fund-raising provides a clear example of this warning. If you're approached by a twenty-five-member organization hoping to raise $50,000 in two months by selling candy door-to-door, decline the honor.

How worthy is the cause in light of overall community concern? When the community seriously needs a new truck for the volunteer fire company, don't get involved with a drive to fund new playground equipment. Above all, if the cause is actually or potentially controversial, stay away from it. This means almost all political or social issues. If you are interested in these issues, don't involve yourself too openly and don't involve your business at all.

Try to be the "big" sponsor. Although you should be cautious about committing too much time or hard cash, there may be other resources you can donate and still be perceived as the main sponsor of a project or event. You might offer your restaurant as the location of project-related activities, assign employees to project work during slack time, donate merchandise, or mention the project in some of your routine advertising. If possible, try to negotiate participation to the exclusion of your major competition.

Come up with your own cause! Although most reasonable opportunities for community involvement stem from fund raising, alternative courses may be open if you look around for them. Is there a problem with youthful vandalism in your community? Perhaps you could spearhead a campaign to reach high-school students through films and talks on the real costs of vandalism. At the same time you could start a community-wide awareness program, including setting up a police hot-line to report acts of vandalism anonymously. Acting as the spokesperson for such activities can give you many chances for favorable press coverage. Is your town a sound candidate for designation as an all-American city? You could spark a move to apply to the National Municipal League for this honor. In other words, use your imagination and your knowledge of the community to come up with a valuable and visible contribution requiring a relatively small expenditure of time and money.

Estimate the return on your investment! It is difficult to place a precise value on community relations. However, you should at least be able to make a calculated judgment on how to balance your costs—in money, time, and resources—against the value of your involvement. How successful are you in terms of positive public attitudes toward you and your business? One aspect of cost-value determination is implicit in your choice to become involved in one activity rather than another. Weigh your choices carefully and decline participation diplomatically so that you don't gain appreciation from one group while alienating another.

Arranging for Publicity

Arranging publicity for your chosen activity should put you in a position not only to gain support and visibility for the project but to establish contact with your local media. This experience could be a hidden but significant benefit to you and your business. One of the most important things to realize about the community press is that they need you too. As a player on the stage of community life, you're also a newsmaker. The drives, events, and projects you support are community news and form an important part of local media appeal.

You might already know media personnel because you're buying space or air time for advertising. This is especially true in small operations where one staff member may wear several hats: publisher, managing editor, and space seller—or station owner, news director, and time seller. Thus, your access to the publication or station will probably be eased by the fact that you're an advertiser. But that's as far as it should go.

Respect the staff member's responsibilities. *Don't* start a phone call about your plans for an event or project with a reminder about how much advertising you've been doing lately. If the project you're calling on is newsworthy, it will get the coverage it deserves. You'll find that setting a professional tone may benefit you in the long run, especially if you find yourself in a negative situation.

Notice that I mentioned calling rather than sending in a press release. That's because in initial contacts with the local press, the formality of a release on a community project might seem slightly pretentious and may actually be counter-productive. (I'm not against press releases. They have their place and I'll be giving you some guidelines on their preparation and use.)

Do be sure that when you call you have prepared and preferably written down answers to the traditional journalistic questions: who, what, when, where, why and how. (Later, you may also want to send the editor a written summary of the facts.) Use this call to find out the media deadlines for news copy. Write these down too and keep them handy for later use.

Naturally, your initial announcement should be timed to permit enough exposure to spark community interest in the event or project you are supporting. You should follow up with a series of "in-progress" stories and a wrap-up article. For example, in a fund-raising drive you may want to announce committee meetings, appointments, or the attainment of intermediate goals (50 percent of total pledged, etc.). Once the drive is complete, you'll want wrap-up articles (e.g., about a check presentation) including photos.

It is for these follow-up stories that you will want to send or deliver press releases. After your opening or launching story, media staff will be aware of the event or project and should be more receptive to press releases. In fact, because of the thin staffing mentioned earlier, a comprehensive release—with photo supplied—will give the editor or news director the facts even if he or she can't send a reporter to cover an event.

Writing press releases. If you write good business letters, you can write good press releases. The intent is the same: communicating your message and relating a series of facts.

Although local media, particularly newspapers, will often use a press release almost in its entirety, space restrictions may not allow them to do so in every case. Moreover, you may want to send your release to the suburban or regional editions of larger newspapers, where the competition for space will be sharper. Radio news directors typically will not be able to use more than a paragraph or so of material. This is why you should pack the answers to who, what, where, when, why, and how in the first paragraph of your release if at all possible. Details and lists of people should follow. Try to confine the release to a single page.

Note the sample release in Figure 8-1. You will see that a company (or project) name and address, along with a phone number and contact name, are already shown. For most purposes, typing in "For Immediate Release" is sufficient, but you may wish to use a specific date instead. The space between the release line and the text is to allow the editor room to write a headline or the news director to write an introduction for the radio announcer.

Start with a date line (Anytown, U.S.A.). Double space the text to leave room for editing. If you must use more than one page, type "more" at the bottom of the first page. Use only one side of a sheet. Number and identify all pages at the top, as shown, and mark the end of the release with stars or some other symbol.

If you have a good photograph to send with your release, do so. A glossy black and white print is best for reproduction, and the 8-inch-by-10-inch size is desirable for handling and cropping. Do not write on the photo or even on paper placed

---

EAT HERE, INC.
4066 W. Union Avenue
Anytown, Iowa 30431

For further information contact:
Robert D. Jones
(912) 555-1212

FOR IMMEDIATE RELEASE

ANYTOWN (IA.)—Robert D. Jones, owner of the Eat Here Restaurant, at the intersection of N. Union Avenue and Route 66 in Anytown, announced a coupon contest today. All holders of coupons drawn will be . . . etc., etc.

EAT HERE, INC. — 2

Summing up the promotion, Jones emphasized that all cash proceeds would go to Anytown's Central Hospital to buy toys and play equipment for the Pediatric Department's Playroom. "We believe in community action," he said, "and intend to . . . etc., etc."

Figure 8.1 Sample Press Release

over it since this ruins the picture for clear reproduction. On the back of the photo scotch tape a caption that clearly identifies the event pictured and accurately spells the names of any people in the photograph.

Before you send out your release, refer to the media deadline list you made up earlier. Don't crowd the deadline. Deliver the release to the publication or radio station yourself, if this is possible.

DEALING WITH BAD PUBLICITY

No matter how carefully you conduct your business or maintain good relations with the local media, you may find yourself in an adversary position with reporters who sincerely believe they are fulfilling their responsibilities by questioning your operation. As suggested in the beginning of this chapter, it's very easy to find yourself in a difficult position due to the press. Consider these other possibilities:

Example:

A customer purchases a take-out order from your restaurant and finds a mouse inside the container. The customer immediately complains to the manager and then contacts the local paper. The paper runs a negative editorial.

Example:

One of your employees talks to a local reporter and alleges that you "victimize" teenagers by paying sub-minimum wages and harassing them. A newspaper reporter then contacts you for a rebuttal.

Example:

Your restaurant is located at a heavily traveled intersection. During a special promotional event that draws a large crowd, a young child is struck by a car while trying to cross the street to reach *your restaurant*. Prior to the accident, community groups have asked you to do something about the heavy traffic flow created in part by the lack of sufficient access to your business. The press, aware of the complaints, arrives to interview you.

The negative situations I've described can and do occur. But specific remedies are almost impossible to prescribe because personalities and circumstances vary so widely. Using these cases, I will discuss how you can handle your relations with the press.

In the case where the mouse was found, you are at a distinct disadvantage: there is evidence and a hostile editorial has already appeared. Your ability to escape serious business loss will primarily depend on how your operations are already perceived in the community. If you are known and recognized as a good, active, concerned citizen—who normally runs a clean operation—that perception may not immunize you from the problem but it will certainly act to soften the impact on your business.

But there are further elements in this case. Was your manager sufficiently apologetic or did his or her manner prompt the woman to take the story to the press? In other words, are your key people alert to the public relations implication of such a situation? *They should be!*

Why did the editor run a critical article? Perhaps your community standing and reputation left much to be desired and the editor felt justified in using the incident as a focus for other shortcomings in the way you operate.

However, the situation may simply be this: you normally run a good operation; the animal came into your restaurant in a package of containers; the editor decided to make some noise so now you're in the soup. As I've described it now though, it's the editor whose conduct is suspect. Why didn't he or she call to hear your explanation? It's now up to you to call and ask for a meeting. At the meeting, don't storm but be firm.

Press for a retraction, placed in a prominent position; but remember that retractions, no matter how visible, only get a small fraction of the attention that attacks do.

Do your best to establish and sustain a good relationship with the editor. Then, get back about your business—and your community activities.

As for the other two cases, whether or not you are really at fault, you should face the impending interviews in the same way: truthfully. This is the only method. If charges are false, deny them. If there are extenuating circumstances, explain them. If you're at fault, state what you are going to do about it.

Remember, your best protection in any case is a public reputation for good business practice, backed by recognized community service.

special
EVENTS
MEAN
special
business

CHAPTER NINE

YOU will recognize similarities between creating special events and creating the types of promotion and public relations we've already considered. The special event is a focal point for promotion and public relations. It's an important element in your marketing program because it springs from community life and from familiar and cherished celebrations.

OPPORTUNITIES FOR SPECIAL EVENTS

Community-based opportunities for special events include parades, charity bazaars for churches and hospitals, fund raising for volunteer fire departments or recreational facilities for the elderly. Your choice of participation should be based on the public relations criteria detailed in the previous chapter, although your main objective in most of these cases will be promotional (with public relations benefits becoming incidental). Let's move on to some specific examples:

Charity Events

You're planning to expand your product or service line in September. Your community orientation alerts you to the fact that every September there is a fund-raising drive for the volunteer fire department. Here's what you can do.

The idea. Suggest to the fund-raising committee that you will donate a specific dollar amount for each of the "new items" purchased during a given introductory period. If they accept your offer, contact the media jointly, following the phone call and release back-up procedure mentioned previously. Arrange for appropriate newspaper and/or radio advertising that introduces your new product or service and announces the donation offer.

The fire department committee will spread the word through all of their fund-raising activities, creating a pervasive community awareness of your new menu addition and the fact that consumers availing themselves of it will also be contributing to the support of the fire department. This, in turn, should generate traffic and sales for your restaurant. Don't forget to follow-up with a public check presentation ceremony at your restaurant and to provide attendant activity.

The payoff. The results are successful introduction of your new menu, funds for the fire department, and an addition to your reservoir of community good will.

Parade

You would like to generate some additional restaurant traffic. Here's one way that should work for you.

The idea. Enter a float from which coupons or low-cost giveaways are distributed to the crowd.

Have the parade start or end at your restaurant. The resulting crowds should generate additional restaurant traffic. Distribute sweepstakes entry blanks to the crowd along the parade route. Stipulate that to be eligible for the sweepstakes prizes, people must deposit the completed entry forms at your restaurant.

The payoff. Increased traffic will increase sales.

Popular Holidays and Observances

Now, here are some ways you can capitalize on popular holidays or observances.

Mother's Day. Contact a local florist and arrange to buy flowers at a discount, then distribute the flowers to women visiting your restaurant or making a specified minimum purchase. You may also manage to obtain the flowers by bartering with the florist for promotion advertising in your restaurant or in the ads you run to publicize the give-away.

St. Patrick's Day. Offer a special discount to anyone wearing green or with an Irish surname.

Valentine's Day. Arrange a tie-in with a local movie to provide a special discount for those buying dinners-for-two at your restaurant. Distribute the discounted tickets to customers who spend a specified or minimum amount for dinner.

Anniversaries. The various anniversaries of your business provide you with excellent promotional opportunities, whether you are celebrating its first, fifth, tenth or fiftieth year of existence. The first thing to remember is that the anniversary should not be confined to one day. You may want to plan celebration events for up to two weeks. Among the promotional devices you may wish to use are across-the-board price roll-backs. For example, if it's your tenth anniversary, you may want to offer selected items at what they would have cost ten years ago. During the celebration period you can distribute to customers coupons that are redeemable after the celebration period is over. You can run a sweepstakes two weeks prior to the anniversary. You can put any number of imaginative promotional tools to work for you during your anniversary celebration.

You can maximize the impact of any special event by planned applications of the various promotional tools and activities already discussed in this book. Be sure that you support the event with adequate media coverage and advertising—nobody can be attracted by your promotion if you don't let them know there *is* a promotion.

how to
face
new
competition
and win

cHApTER TEN

PROPERLY planned promotions will also help you confront one of the more unpleasant realities of business life—new competition. Although a history of successful promotions and recognized community involvement will give you a good foundation for facing competition, you must also be prepared to take action directly aimed at defusing competitive threats. Don't forget: A competitor builds *his business* by taking away *your customers*.

No matter how strong your community image or how loyal your customers, the novelty of a new business and the natural curiosity and attention it attracts makes your business vulnerable. Don't be complacent! Don't think that there's "enough business to go around." Your trading area has its limits for customer potential and a new operation may easily absorb any slack. But the newcomer's success will depend on making inroads into *your* sales and profits.

As a neighborhood-restaurant operator you will know enough about what is going on in your trading area so that no competition, whether an individual operation or chain branch, will be able to get very far with their plans before you find out about them. And, when you do find out, *Act!* Start planning a counteroffensive immediately.

PLANNING A COMPETITIVE STRATEGY

Your aim should be to retain—not regain. You should start your campaign by taking a hard, critical, and thorough look at every aspect of your business, from product mix to operations to marketing. Then compare your business to the new competition so that you have a complete understanding of your relative strengths and weaknesses. Keep yourself informed of the competition's plans for operation and opening strategy.

Meet with your staff, from managers and bookkeepers to salespeople. Explain the competitive situation and enlist their aid in preparing your strategy. At least two months before your competitor opens his or her doors, hold a refresher course with those employees who deal directly with the customers. Concentrate on courtesy, efficiency, prompt service.

Remember the old line, "I'll take my business elsewhere"; and remember that the disgruntled customer will soon have an "elsewhere" within easy reach. The "elsewhere" may be shiny new and have the benefits of the latest technology—computerized cash registers ready to flash business that used to be yours on their display screens. The "elsewhere" may be well-publicized and ready to attract your customers with Grand Opening Celebration promotions and fanfare. Prepare your operation so that you're ready to cope with the actuality of competition.

The Importance of Timing

In all likelihood you won't be able to match the money and energy that the competition will expend on opening activity. Moreover, you have to face the unpleasant fact that most people, even your most loyal customers, will be tempted by the opportunity to try something new. Any promotion you run during the opening and immediately after (during post-opening activities) may be weakened by that natural temptation. So, don't give your customers any added excuse or reason to exercise their curiosity. Use the opening and *pre*-opening periods to reinforce your community involvement. Continue to run inexpensive promotions aimed at increasing customer frequency and loyalty.

You should also use your competitor's opening and post-opening periods—four to six weeks—to shop the operation to assess more accurately his or her strengths and weaknesses. Prepare marketing plans based on your realistic observations.

Then, after the competition's opening momentum and expenditures have started to ebb, let loose with a major high-impact, high-visibility marketing plan of your own. Open up with a *direct-response-oriented* program. Then, follow up with the community-oriented programs outlined in Chapter Nine.

I recommend this strategy regardless of the size of your competition and the amount of support (i.e., chain funding) for advertising. You can defeat quantity promotions with quality promotions that are well-timed. In this context I stress my contention that neighborhood-restaurant marketing is the "great equalizer."

Developing Your Strengths

When battling competition, concentrate on the cards in your own hand; they're the ones you have to play. Your strongest card is your own "unique selling proposition." Determine the special differences that place your business above the competition. Consider menu items, special services, decor, or locale.

Ask yourself this question: If a new restaurant opened across the street or in the mall tomorrow, how confident would I be about my current community reputation and marketing posture? Remember that the real way to fight competition is *always* to run your business as if new competition were *right now* planning to invade your trading area!

MOTIVATING YOUR EMPLOYEES TO HIGHER PRODUCTIVITY

CHAPTER ELEVEN

THE last chapter discussed the necessity of reviewing and improving the way your employees treat customers, especially when you are faced with new competition. Yes, you should review service in a crisis; but, you should find little room for improvement. As a restaurant operator, one of your most important jobs is to see that your crew personnel are *properly trained and continually motivated to deliver consistently superior service to your customers.*

It's amazing that so many restaurant operators just don't understand the importance of the salesperson-customer relationship. The same restaurant operator who pays huge sums to outfit his or her store, to advertise and promote goods and services, and to stock quality items and buy the best equipment totally ignores nurturing the most important business asset—those employees who deal with the public.

SERVICE AND CUSTOMER SATISFACTION

Many of these otherwise astute business people suffer from the "silent complaint" syndrome. This business disease is all the more damaging because its very nature is its undetectability.

Here are the painful symptoms: a customer irritated by poor or slow service or surliness leaves the restaurant without complaining to the management and simply never returns. He or she breaks silence only to tell family and friends not to patronize the restaurant. The owner or manager never knows why customers are lost, but the sales charts indicate that the business is ailing.

I have to admit that my sympathy is limited for restaurant operators who allow themselves to be made victims of the "silent complaint" syndrome. It is a situation they bring on themselves by neglecting to administer the proper preventive medicine.

Many negligent restaurant operators defend themselves by claiming that they just can't pay enough to attract quality help. My advice to them is two-fold: Don't stint any more in paying good wages than you would for an advertising or promotional campaign; then, work with your crew to make sure they don't just conduct your business but build it as well.

SUGGESTIONS FOR STAFF MOTIVATION

Now that I've described the disease, I'm going to prescribe some specific treatment—treatment consisting of programs based on different mixtures of these common elements: *communications, group recognition, individual recognition, compensation, pride of performance,* and *team spirit.* Naturally, you'll adapt these programs to the size and nature of your operation.

PROGRAM
Employee-of-the-Month

Objective: To motivate individual performance.

This program is designed to recognize the top performer on your restaurant staff each month. You should make sure that the criteria are prominently posted and that any new employees know that the program exists. Although you will want to choose standards tailored to the needs of your restaurant, here are some general standards you may choose from: punctuality, appearance, attitude, and job performance. As an alternative, you may wish to have all employees vote for the top performer of the month.

The winning crew member should receive cash, a savings bond, or tickets to a special event: a play, a football game, etc. The prize should be worth winning because it is, after all, a form of bonus compensation. To further enhance the program, display a plaque with each monthly winner's name entered on it as a constant incentive to all crew members.

PROGRAM
Employee "Family Album" or Newsletter

Objective: To promote team spirit and morale.

Appoint an employee committee to compile an album about your restaurant or select an employee to "publish" a typewritten and photocopied monthly or semi-monthly newsletter. Here are some sample entries:

- Newspaper Stories about the Restaurant
- Promotion Information
- Marketing Program Information
- Store Sporting or Social Events
- Articles about Individual Accomplishments
- Employee-of-the-Month Announcements

The newsletter is also a good vehicle for training and motivational tips from management.

PROGRAM
Employee Meetings

Objective: To promote positive and open communication between management and staff.

Regularly scheduled meetings, perhaps with coffee and soft drinks being served, give employees a chance to air grievances constructively, to ask questions, or make suggestions to help the business. You or your manager can take the opportunity to talk about general operations, promotions, or items you view as problems. The important thing to remember about such meetings is that they shouldn't be used as occasions of public chastisement or humiliation—management should be prepared to *talk with, not down to* the staff. For these meetings to be effective, employees should be *able to look forward to them, not dread them.* You may choose to set up an informal crew member committee to recommend topics for discussion.

PROGRAM

Refer a Friend

Objective: To involve your staff in helping you to find other good people.

This program is intended to assist you in recruiting qualified personnel. Current employees are offered a cash bonus for applicants that you actually hire. The program can be run as a contest with the winner being the employee who suggested the most hired applicants —or with each employee being rewarded individually for every recommended applicant hired.

PROGRAM

Mystery Shopper

Objective: To monitor employee performance.

Engage a "Shopper Service" or someone your regular employees do not know to pose as a regular customer.

The mystery shopper should evaluate the employee on certain specific criteria you have set for performance, for example, courtesy, knowledge, side-order selling, or proper cash handling procedures.

If the employee meets all of these criteria, he or she should be immediately awarded a $5 or $10 cash bonus. If the employee does not satisfy all criteria, he should be given a card saying "You goofed" with the appropriate criteria checked to show where the failure occurred. You should study overall results for trends.

PROGRAM

"Score a Touchdown"

Objective: To increase sales or product mix units.

This program involves a contest in which crew members try to meet a specific goal set by management.

This goal can be a general sales increase or one based on raw units of one or more products. It should be based on previous restaurant performance. Once the goal is set, it should be divided into steps, with each step being converted into a certain amount of yards as on a football field. For example, if the goal is to increase sales by $1,000, then each $100 increase would represent a ten-yard advance. If the goal is achieved, a touchdown is scored and the entire staff is rewarded. A graduated prize schedule should be created to reward the staff if they achieve over 50 percent but not 100 percent.

For example:
    Progress to—50 yard line—$ 5
                40 yard line—$10
                30 yard line—$20
                20 yard line—$30
                10 yard line—$40
            Touchdown —$50
                Total—$155

PROGRAM

Neighborhood Flyer Distribution

Objective: To build employee involvement and sales.

Select streets in your trading area for distribution of a flyer containing a special offer or discount coupon. Divide your crew members into teams, with each team receiving a different colored flyer for distribution to a designated area (the offer is the same). After distribution is completed, post a chart in the restaurant showing flyer redemption by team-color. Award prizes to the team achieving the highest number of flyers redeemed.

This program can run as a competition between individuals as well as on a team basis. Award weekly prizes in addition to the grand prize to maintain interest throughout the competition's duration.

THE CREW AND CUSTOMER CONTACT

If, as you've been reading these program suggestions, you've felt that *you* don't need to worry about your employees or that the programs don't seem to be worth the bother, let me make a few further points.

First, your restaurant's staff personifies your advertising image. In most cases, your crew members are the public's *only* point of direct contact with your business. Customers or prospective customers rarely have the chance to talk with your management or the people responsible for your advertising or marketing. Your crew members are the ones who fulfill or fail to fulfill your advertising promise. Moreover, they can ruin in an instant the business image you've worked for years to build.

Second, good marketing can kill a bad operation. What this adage means is that if you are successful in promoting business and your crew members do not deliver good, prompt, and courteous service, your restaurant will suffer even more than if you neglected promotion entirely.

Third, once customers are turned off by an employee, you will have to spend two or three times more money, time, and effort to lure them back—resources that could have gone to attracting new customers.

Finally, to touch realistically on a sensitive subject: employees are far less likely to steal from an employer who treats them fairly, shows concern for their wants and needs, and involves them in the business.

For these four reasons and others given before, it is wise to invest your resources in training and motivating your crew members. Properly treated, they can be your best business asset. Conversely, they can be your worst liability. The choice is largely up to you.

NEIGHBORHOOD-RESTAURANT MARKETING REPRESENTATIVE

I think I can assume that by now you've absorbed and appreciated the philosophy of neighborhood-restaurant marketing.

For the most part, I've talked about putting that philosophy into action yourself or enlisting the part-time assistance of your crew members. However, it may be that your operations are of such a scope or in such need of concentrated neighborhood-restaurant marketing that you may wish to take a further step. You may want to assign someone on your staff to take on full time, or nearly full time, the duties of a Neighborhood-Restaurant Marketing Representative. You may want to go so far as to recruit someone specifically to do this job for you. I'd advise you to consider this possibility very seriously if you have more than one restaurant. And, if you do decide that an N-RM representative will help your business, be extremely selective about the qualifications of the person you assign or hire.

The prime requirement for your N-RM representative is the capability to understand neighborhood-restaurant marketing as described in this book and to execute its programs accordingly. In short, he or she must be able to do all the things set forth in the past eleven chapters of this book.

This means that to a great extent you will be choosing a stand-in for yourself in devising, planning, and carrying out neighborhood-restaurant marketing from situation analysis through employee motivation. Choose carefully. Once again, your business could be at stake. Here are some of the attributes you should look for in a prospective N-RM representative and the type of person most likely to have them:

1. *Maturity.* A person with common sense and the ability to apply it in all types of situations and with all kinds of people.
2. *Personality.* The extrovert who can effortlessly and naturally project enthusiasm and invite others to share that enthusiasm.
3. *Self-Starting Self-Confidence.* The go-getter who will act on his or her own decisions and knowledge. Once trained in N-RM perspective and techniques, this person should be able to set the promotional pace and tenor of your business.
4. *Reliability.* The detail worker who plans thoroughly and thoughtfully lays out every aspect of a task

in careful detail and then follows each detail down
to its planned conclusion.

You should first seek your N-RM representative from among your own employees. This course of action has several advantages. Not only will you have someone whose qualities you already know, but someone who knows the basics of your business. Because the assignment should be considered a promotion and should rate a raise to emphasize its importance and excite enthusiasm, it will also open the prospect of advancement to other employees—a morale booster in itself.

No matter where you find your neighborhood-restaurant marketing representative, you should take several steps to assure that the job is clearly defined as to objectives and reporting structure. In addition to executing the primary tasks described in this book, which should be studied by the representative as a training manual, the representative can function as a liaison between management and other personnel in matters relating to the operational and promotional aspects of marketing and advertising programs.

The N-RM representative should also be charged with laying out promotional plans extending over a year, with activities broken out according to quarters. At the end of each quarter, you should review with the representative the status of programs in progress and approve recommendations for upcoming quarters.

Appointing a neighborhood-restaurant marketing representative, like embracing the N-RM philosophy itself, is a long-term investment. The results may not be immediate in either case, but you will have laid a strong foundation for an ongoing, smooth-running, and profit-oriented marketing program that will increase the value of all the efforts and energies you have devoted to building your restaurant business.

maximizing the sales potential of special markets

chapter twelve

THROUGHOUT this book the principles and tactics of neighborhood-restaurant marketing have been discussed as they apply to "normal" community situations. But neighborhood-restaurant marketing, with focused modification, is also extremely potent in building sales at special locations: shopping malls, urban (dense daytime population of workers) centers, interstate highway exit-access sites, drive-throughs, and at restaurants that serve particular population concentrations.

In all these cases, you must take the same care to turn all of my seven keys as you would for any other foodservice unit. But you must be alert to some different opportunities to take fullest advantage of their natural sales potential. And, you must be prepared to overcome different sales obstacles.

Although dozens of pages might be filled with specific recommendations for optimizing sales in particular restaurant types and market segments, I'm going to assume that you've become sufficiently familiar with the tenets of neighborhood-restaurant marketing to be ready to handle these specialized circumstances with discipline and continuity. However, I'd like to give you some idea of the kinds of things you may want to make part of your overall program for these facilities.

SHOPPING MALLS

In shopping malls, for instance, be aware that you have two on-site sets of customers—those who work for stores operating at the mall and those who shop at these stores. For workers you might want to initiate a delivery service to lounge areas or feature "before the mall opens" breakfasts. You can salute a different business in the mall each week with a free food day for their employees; or you can arrange with other mall businesses to stuff your restaurant's "coupon offers" in their pay envelopes.

Because the traditional exterior sign is not usually allowable at malls, you may want to improvise by having decorated cars or vehicles in the parking lot, preferably near the entrance, to create immediate awareness among entering shoppers. You may want to provide strollers for shoppers with children. Be sure that you are prominently represented on information kiosks. If there is a movie in the mall, you can tie-in a coupon handout at the theatre to attract after-show snackers or diners. Be aware that Sunday is a big family day at malls. Make the Sunday papers available with "brunch"; tie-in with church groups; and offer space for flower shows, antique shows, or other browsing attractions.

Is there a central screen for mall commercials? Make sure you're on it. And, mall regulations permitting, consider the possibility of opening a "sidewalk cafe" outside your restaurant.

DRIVE-THROUGHS

If you have a drive-through operation, don't regard it as simply an outside counter. For starters, be sure to mention your drive-through as a distinct attraction in all of your general advertising Then, remember that to really build your sales you should ccncentrate on promotions that really pitch the availability and advantages of your operation.

Use direct-mail coupons specifically for drive-through redemption. Use other store operations to promote drive-through usage, from P.O.P. materials to bagstuffers for walk-in-carry-out-customers. Cross-promote with other drive-in facilities such as cleaners, banks, gas stations, and movies to attract people who are already in their cars. Make sure that your drive-through is properly lighted for both advertisement and security.

Once people have joined the line of cars at your drive-through, don't just let them sit and wait. Of course, they should *never* wait long, because speed is the name of the drive-through game. However, you can take the sting out of any wait by having a crew member wipe off windshields or hand out balloons, other premiums, or coupons to children in the vehicle. A crew member can be assigned as an outside order taker.

INTERSTATE SITES

Because interstate sites and drive-throughs (they are often profitably combined) share many characteristics, they also share similar promotional potential. For instance, premiums at either type of restaurant might include coloring books to entertain kids or towelettes to keep them clean. Adult customers would appreciate change holders, note pads, key chains, litter bags, and the like.

There are many ways to pull traffic into your restaurant on the interstate, from using signs (as prominent as local ordinances allow) to cross-promotions with other interstate units. You might want to consider staying open for twenty-four hours to attract bus business or you might want to contact local schools to entice bus groups to stop at your restaurant after athletic events. It may be advantageous to tie-in with nearby camping grounds or any resorts, including ski lodges and the like. Network radio advertising during peak seasons may also be helpful. Don't forget that most interstates are near towns and that neighborhood-restaurant marketing techniques should be employed religiously to attract patronage from those towns.

URBAN RESTAURANTS

Urban restaurants, too, have some distinctive traits. The most obvious is that operators of such restaurants have to be ready to cater to and attract individual adults rather than family groups. A large majority of urban customers walk to your restaurant; and the likelihood is strong that they are often going to be tempted to simply walk into a competitor who is just slightly closer to the place where they are working or shopping. So, you have to provide a greater attraction to your restaurant, whether it's faster service, for those who just want a bite before using the rest of their lunch hour for shopping, or individual seating arrangements, for those who may cherish lunchtime as a time for some relative privacy.

SPECIAL CONSIDERATIONS

I think that these examples will give you a good idea of how to treat special restaurant types in a special way. The same holds true for special types of population concentrations. You may want to modify your menu according to group preferences. Also, if you play music in your unit, you will want to make selections that will make your customers feel comfortable. If you're trying to attract senior citizens, you don't want to play rock and roll.

SUMMARY

But all these examples are traceable to the same fundamentals. You must know your customers and your locations. To increase your market penetration and to build sales you must be adaptable and flexible in your choice of promotions. And you must, naturally, back up your promotions with timely, well coordinated services and operations.

Go get 'em—With neighborhood-restaurant marketing!!!

index